THE

Summer

Pudding Club

BOOK

Keith and Jean Turner have both had varied careers. Between them they have been school teacher, dental surgeon, personnel manager, farmer and marriage counsellor, as well as raising a large family. They were hoteliers for many years during which they optimistically founded the Pudding Club. They were delighted that their enthusiasm was not misplaced and that the Pudding Club is such a success.

Mary Stokes was chef at the Three Ways hotel in Mickleton where the Pudding Club was founded. When the hotel introduced its Summer Pudding Club parties, she won acclaim with a repertoire of delicious summer desserts. She now advises hotels and restaurants on food management.

Also by Keith and Jean Turner
(with Annette Balfour Lynn)

The Pudding Club Book

THE *Summer Pudding Club* BOOK

Keith and Jean Turner

WITH

Mary Stokes

FOREWORD

BY

Chris Kelly

HEADLINE

First published in 1999
by HEADLINE BOOK PUBLISHING

First published in softback in 2000
by HEADLINE BOOK PUBLISHING

10 9 8 7 6 5 4 3 2 1

ISBN 0 7472 7552 1

Designed by Peter Ward
Typeset by Letterpart Limited, 16 Bell street, Reigate, Surrey
Printed and bound in Great Britain by
Butler & Tanner Ltd, Frome and London

HEADLINE BOOK PUBLISHING
A division of the Hodder Headline Group
338 Euston Road
London NW1 3BH

www.headline.co.uk
www.hodderheadline.com

CONTENTS

FOREWORD

THE SUCCESS of the first Pudding Club book proved something we've all suspected from the cradle: that Britain and pudding are synonymous. It confirmed that pudding is as much part of the British psyche as stubby little family saloons (now, alas, German or Japanese and distressingly stylish), shapeless Harris tweed jackets and the shipping forecast. The battle of Waterloo wasn't won on the playing fields of Eton at all. It was won in the good old draughty British kitchen, where the pudding production line wrought far more havoc on the enemy than any amount of shells and bayonets. It was our substantial puddings that gave our soldiers heart; that drove them on to deeds of indescribable daring; that put the fear of God into the French, a nation sent to war on nothing more sustaining than goats' milk cheese. By rights, Shakespeare should have written about 'this sceptred pudding', so integral a part of our national genius is that unique confection.

Has it ever occurred to you to wonder why no British team has won the World Cup, or indeed anything else much, since 1966? After profound research I've come to a startling conclusion. It's because round about the late sixties we turned our collective back on pudding. Egged on by resentfully thin magazine editors, and frightened witless by reports of heart disease epidemics, overnight we turned into a bunch of mewling wimps. Where once we would have dug with a will into the ginger sponge or the roly-poly, now we even rudely refused the lemon tart at dinner parties, reciting what was to become the world's most boring mantra: 'Just coffee for me, please.'

The result, apart from the death of laughter and good conversation, and a worrying tendency to compensate by drinking twice as much, was that our sportsmen and women became so enfeebled they practically lost the use of their limbs. Strikers fainted as they approached the penalty spot, and tennis players had bigger rackets made to reduce the necessary effort. Our traditional opponents, meanwhile, had the good sense to remain life conscious rather than simply health conscious. Tell Shane Warne pudding's bad for you and he'd call you a pommie four X.

A nation, I concluded, turns its back on pudding at its peril. And that's why I rejoice at pudding's comeback, a glorious renaissance with the visionaries of the Pudding Club indisputably in the vanguard. But we have more to thank them for than simply the restoration of a national treasure. Thanks to their untiring efforts, and the resulting appetite for afters, our sporting prowess is once again the envy of the world. Only recently we were placed fourth at the International Pigeon Fanciers' Convention in Belgium, and in Wolverhampton we trounced Europe's best at Scrabble.

Speaking personally, pudding didn't have to make a comeback for me. It never went away. I love it in all its luxury, variety, colour, texture and sensuality. It is infinitely versatile, as this splendid collection amply demonstrates. Designed for summer, these recipes leave behind the more robust creations of the cold months, and introduce lighter, more succulent, perhaps more feminine puddings; puddings that rely as much on the garden as on ingredients in packets.

And it's not just eating I enjoy. When my wife and I cook together, the puddings are my contribution. There is about this arrangement more than a touch of selfishness on my part. Like the last, climactic act in a play – or perhaps in this case more aptly a musical – the pudding is the course that, if you get it right, sends the audience home glowing with what Ken Dodd calls 'plumptiousness'.

In these pages you'll find unparalleled opportunities for fostering plumptiousness. And as you joyfully cook, remember that in doing so you're helping to bring the glittering prizes back to Britain!

CHRIS KELLY

INTRODUCTION
TO THE
Summer Pudding Club

THIS BOOK would never have come about had it not been for a fine example of British obstinacy, when in true bulldog fashion there was a refusal to let go. This was back in the 1980s, a couple of years after we had started our Pudding Club meetings at the Three Ways House Hotel in Mickleton. The meetings were held twice a month, during the winter, with a break in the months of June, July and August, because we had assumed that no one would want to come and eat puddings in the summer.

So, a tribute is due to those fervent pudding-lovers who refused to accept this interruption of their pleasure. 'But you can't possibly eat hot and sticky puddings in the summer months,' we said. 'Oh yes, you can,' they said. 'Oh no, you can't,' we said – in true pantomime style – and there we might have been stuck, had not someone spoken up and pointed out that here was an opportunity to tackle the national repertoire of wonderful summery puddings.

Thanks to that inspiration, the convivial and zestful gatherings of pudding-lovers became a year-round feature of life at the Three Ways. Weather permitting, we assembled out on the terrace for our aperitifs, and these summer meetings became known as 'Summer Pudding Patio Parties'. Apart from that, and the sort of puddings on offer, the evenings followed the formula of the established (winter) Pudding Club meetings – no starter, a choice of mains (with a warning to leave space for the puds) and then unlimited access to seven suitably varied but equally naughty creations.

Initially, we were unsure whether there would be the same variety of summery puddings available as there were hot and sticky ones. We need not have worried – we soon discovered that this country has a wide range of summery desserts, many of them dating from before the days of freezers and refrigerators and all of them worthy of being preserved and celebrated anew. The Summer Pudding Club quickly became an established feature in the Pudding Club's calendar.

The chef at the Three Ways at that time was Mary Stokes, and her skill and knowledge became as important to the Summer Pudding Club as to the winter one. Like us, Mary has moved on from the Three Ways House Hotel, and now lives and works in the Scottish Highlands. Notwithstanding that, she did not hesitate when we sought her help with the production of this book. Immediately, she came forward not only with suggestions, but with recipes too, and once again we had reason to marvel at her ability to achieve wonders with no obvious effort and absolutely no fuss. To a large degree, this is her book.

Our thanks are also due to the new owners of the Three Ways House Hotel, Peter Henderson and Simon Coombe, for the way the Pudding Club has continued to thrive there. Their ideas and enthusiasm will, we are sure, ensure the club's growth and development.

Except where indicated, medium eggs should be used.

KEITH AND JEAN TURNER

CHAPTER ONE
Quick and Easy

T HE RECIPES in this section are really generous – in the sense
that, having made them, you will find that the results go far
beyond the time and effort involved in their preparation. But be
careful: while they are all easy to make and involve very little
preparation time, they are not necessarily 'quick' in the sense of
being ready for the table in five minutes. Some of them require
time in the oven or the fridge – even overnight – but that doesn't
stop them being amazingly quick and easy.

Raspberries with Yoghurt

A simple but delicious dessert, which could also be made with strawberries, redcurrants or blackberries. It looks nice served in tall wine glasses, decorated with mint leaves.

Serves 4-6

450G (1 LB) RASPBERRIES	570ML (1 PINT) NATURAL GREEK
CLEAR HONEY TO TASTE	YOGHURT

Remove the stalks and leaves from the raspberries. (If you are using strawberries, halve or quarter them.) Chill the prepared fruit. Stir the honey into the Greek yoghurt, adjusting the quantities according to taste. Layer the fruit and yoghurt in individual glasses. Serve very cold.

Cranachan

A tasty and traditional Scottish dessert, cranachan can be made with raspberries or with chopped strawberries.

Serves 4

125G (4½ OZ) COARSE OATMEAL	150G (5 OZ) RASPBERRIES, CUT
400ML (14 FL OZ) DOUBLE CREAM	INTO PIECES
50G (2 OZ) CASTER SUGAR	A FEW WHOLE RASPBERRIES AND
WHISKY, RUM OR ORANGE	MINT LEAVES, OR GRATED
LIQUEUR	CHOCOLATE TO DECORATE

Preheat the oven to 200°C/400°F/Gas 6.

Place the oatmeal on a baking tray and lightly brown. Shake the tray occasionally to allow the oatmeal to brown evenly.

Whip the cream until stiff, then stir in the oatmeal, sugar and alcohol.

Stir in the fruit, or layer the cream mixture and fruit. Spoon into individual glass dishes and top with one or two whole raspberries and mint leaves, or a little grated chocolate.

Note

You can usually find oatmeal in supermarkets or health shops. Please do not use porridge oats.

Butterscotch Pudding

An old-fashioned dessert, made with ingredients that you are likely to find to hand in your kitchen cupboard. Try it with one of the ice-cream sauces (pages 73-75).

Serves 4-6

25G (1 OZ) CORNFLOUR	25G (1 OZ) BUTTER
500ML (17 FL OZ) CREAMY MILK	5ML (1 TSP) VANILLA ESSENCE
2 EGGS, SEPARATED	25G (1 OZ) WALNUTS, CHOPPED,
110G (4 OZ) SOFT BROWN SUGAR	TO DECORATE

In a large bowl, mix the cornflour with a little of the milk to a paste. Bring the remaining milk to a boil and pour gradually on to the cornflour paste, stirring constantly to prevent lumpiness.

Return the mixture to a clean pan and bring to a simmer, stirring all the time. Simmer for 2-3 minutes, then remove from the heat and cool for 5 minutes. Add the egg yolks to the pan and stir thoroughly. Cook without boiling for 2-3 minutes.

Dissolve the sugar in a heavy-based saucepan and add the butter. When the butter has melted, stir into the cornflour sauce. In another bowl, whisk the egg whites until stiff and fold into the pudding mix. Add the vanilla essence. Pour into a serving dish and refrigerate for 2 hours. Decorate with chopped walnuts.

Note

If your milk and cornflour mixture does become lumpy, simply whizz it all up in a liquidizer or food processor until smooth.

Chocolate Pavé

Chocoholics will love this very rich recipe. Pavé is a French term meaning paving slab. It is delicious served with fresh raspberries, or strawberries, and cream. Or try it with one of the ice-cream sauces (pages 73-75).

Serves 4-6

350G (12 OZ) GOOD QUALITY PLAIN CHOCOLATE	3 EGG YOLKS
100ML (3½ FL OZ) STRONG BLACK COFFEE	275ML (½ PINT) WHIPPING OR DOUBLE CREAM

Break the chocolate into pieces and place them, with the coffee, in a bowl over a pan of simmering water. When the chocolate has melted, allow the mixture to cool slightly and then beat in the egg yolks, one at a time. Whip the cream until it holds its shape – not too stiff. Fold it into the chocolate mixture.

Prepare a 450g (1 lb) loaf tin by lining it with clingfilm. The mixture can be poured into a bowl or individual glasses if you don't possess a loaf tin. Pour the mixture into the lined loaf tin or glasses, and refrigerate until it is needed.

Brandy Whip

This recipe is so simple; it can be served on its own with biscuits, or with a bowl of freshly prepared soft fruits.

Serves 4-6

400ML (14 FL OZ) DOUBLE CREAM	CASTER SUGAR (OPTIONAL)
100ML (3½ FL OZ) BRANDY	GROUND NUTMEG, TO TASTE
JUICE OF ½ LEMON	(OPTIONAL)

In a large bowl, whip the cream to soft peaks, then add the brandy and lemon juice. Taste, and add sugar and nutmeg if required. Spoon the mixture into individual glasses or a large serving bowl, and refrigerate.

Variation

Use half cream and half thick creamy yoghurt and add runny honey to taste. Spoon the mixture into a heat-resistant dish, cover thickly with demerara sugar and place under a hot grill until the sugar has caramelized. Chill.

Baked Stuffed Peaches

A traditional Italian dessert. If you use nectarines instead of peaches you won't have to remove the skins.

Serves 4

1 TBSP UNSALTED BUTTER, SOFTENED	50G (2 OZ) AMARETTI OR RATAFIA BISCUITS, CRUMBLED
2 DSTSP CASTOR SUGAR	4 LARGE RIPE PEACHES OR NECTARINES
1 EGG YOLK	

Preheat the oven to 180°C/350°F/Gas 4.

Cream together the butter and sugar, add the egg yolk and stir in the crumbled Amaretti or ratafia biscuits.

If you're using peaches, place them in a pan and cover with boiling water. Leave for 2-3 minutes, pour off the water and peel off the skins. Halve the peaches or nectarines and remove the stones. Enlarge the cavities by scooping out some of the flesh with a teaspoon and add the pulp to the biscuit mixture.

Pile the biscuit stuffing into the peach halves and arrange in a lightly buttered ovenproof dish. Bake in the oven for 20-30 minutes, until the peaches are soft but still holding their shape. Serve warm with cream or ice-cream.

Bakewell Pudding

Usually called Bakewell Tart, but it should properly be referred to as a pudding. If you buy a reputable brand of ready-made pastry, this really will make it a quickly prepared dessert.

Serves 4-6

175G–225G (6-8 OZ) PUFF OR SHORTCRUST PASTRY	4 EGGS
RASPBERRY JAM	125G (4½ OZ) CASTER SUGAR
125G (4½ OZ) BUTTER	125G (4½ OZ) GROUND ALMONDS

Preheat the oven to 200-220⁰C/400-425⁰F/Gas 6-7.

Roll out the pastry and line a 20cm (8 in) tart tin. Spread the jam over the base. Melt the butter and leave to cool slightly. Beat the eggs and sugar to a pale, thick cream. Slowly pour in the butter, stirring, then fold in the almonds. Turn into the prepared pastry case. Bake in the oven for 20-40 minutes, depending on the depth of your pudding. The pudding is ready when it feels just firm. Alternatively, test the pudding with a skewer – when the skewer comes out clean the pudding is ready. Serve warm with cream.

Variation

Delicious if you replace the jam with a layer of fresh raspberries, sprinkled with a little caster sugar.

Vanilla Cream

Lovely served with fresh berries and a fruit sauce. Delicious with chocolate sauce, too.

Serves 4-6

425ML (¾ PINT) WHIPPING CREAM	425ML (¾ PINT) THICK CREAMY
11G (1½ X 0.4 OZ) SACHETS OF	YOGHURT
GELATINE POWDER	2 TSP VANILLA ESSENCE
75G (3 OZ) CASTER SUGAR	

Put 3 tablespoons of the cream in a small bowl, sprinkle on the gelatine, stir and leave to soak for 10 minutes. Put the remaining cream and sugar in a pan and gently bring to a simmer (but don't allow it to boil). Stir in the soaked gelatine and whisk over the heat for a few seconds. Remove from the heat.

In a large bowl, stir the yoghurt and vanilla essence together, then pour in the cream mixture through a sieve and stir thoroughly. Pour into individual glass bowls or into a 450g (1 lb) loaf tin lined with clingfilm. Cover and allow to set for 4-6 hours.

Fruit Sauce

225G (8 OZ) BLACKCURRANTS,	STRAWBERRIES (OR A MIXTURE)
REDCURRANTS, RASPBERRIES OR	50-75G (2-3 OZ) CASTER SUGAR

Simply whizz all the fruit up together, then sieve. Test for sweetness and add sugar to taste.

Blackcurrant Fool

One of the best recipes for a 'fool'. Serve with Popcorn Biscuits (see page 83) or Ginger Crisps (see page 82).

Serves 4-6

50G (2 OZ) UNSALTED BUTTER	275ML (½ PINT) DOUBLE OR
450G (I LB) BLACKCURRANTS	WHIPPING CREAM
CASTER SUGAR, TO TASTE	

Melt the butter in a large pan, then add the blackcurrants. Cover and leave to cook gently for about 10 minutes, shaking the pan occasionally. When the fruit has softened, remove from the heat and crush the fruit with a wooden spoon, then a fork. The fruit needs to be crushed, not puréed. Add sugar to taste. Allow to cool.

Whip the cream until firm and fold it into the fruit. Serve lightly chilled.

Variations

Fools can also be made with rhubarb, blackberry and apple, gooseberry and apricot.

Wine and Honey Syllabub

Syllabubs were being made as early as the seventeenth century. Serve with home-made or good quality bought biscuits.

Serves 4-6

2 TBSP CLEAR HONEY	275ML (½ PINT) DOUBLE CREAM
6 TBSP DRY WHITE WINE	I TBSP TOASTED ALMONDS OR
I TBSP BRANDY (OPTIONAL)	HAZELNUTS, CHOPPED, TO
2 TSP GRATED LEMON RIND	DECORATE
JUICE OF ½ LEMON	

In a large bowl, mix the honey, wine, brandy (if using), lemon rind and juice and leave, preferably for a few hours or overnight. Add the cream and whisk until you have a soft bulky whiteness. Spoon into individual wine glasses and scatter with nuts to decorate.

Note

If you only have thick honey, simply heat it gently until it runs clear.

CHAPTER TWO

Pudding Club Winners

A<small>T THE</small> Summer Pudding Club, as at the winter club, the evening ends with a vote to establish the most popular pudding of the evening. Everyone attending has just one vote to cast for his or her favourite. (There is an exception to the rule, in that if you have had more than one helping of the pudding of your choice, you can have as many votes as you have had helpings!) The puddings in this section have each achieved the distinction of being voted 'Pudding of the Evening'.

Chocolate and Raspberry Roulade

It really isn't easy to make a smaller version of this pudding, but if there is any left at the end of the meal, it does freeze well.

Serves 6-8

6 LARGE EGGS, SEPARATED	225G (8 OZ) FRESH RASPBERRIES,
225G (8 OZ) CASTER SUGAR	CHOPPED, AND A FEW WHOLE
50G (2 OZ) COCOA POWDER	ONES, TO DECORATE
425ML (¾ PINT) DOUBLE OR	MINT LEAVES, TO DECORATE
WHIPPING CREAM	

Preheat the oven to 180°C/350°F/Gas 4.

Lightly oil and line a Swiss-roll tin, approximately 30 x 20 x 2.5cm (12 x 8 x 1 in) with parchment or greaseproof paper.

Beat the egg yolks until they thicken and are pale in colour. Add the sugar and beat briefly again. Stir in the cocoa powder. In a separate bowl, beat the egg whites until they are stiff but not dry. Gently fold the cocoa mixture into the egg whites. Pour into the prepared tin and bake in the oven for 20 minutes, or until springy to the touch.

Meanwhile, in a clean bowl, whisk the cream until it forms stiff peaks.

Allow the cake to cool in the tin before turning it out on to a sheet of greaseproof paper dusted with caster sugar. Cover with the whipped cream, reserving some for decoration, and the chopped raspberries. Roll it up and flip it on to a plate. Pipe with the reserved cream and decorate with the whole raspberries and mint leaves.

Note

Parchment paper, available in most supermarkets, is 100 per cent non-stick.

Variation

For extra chocolatiness, melt 225g (8 oz) of plain chocolate and spread on to the cake before adding the cream.
Fill with chopped strawberries instead of the raspberries.

Chocolate Bombe

A very popular and impressive-looking dessert that is a frequent winner at the Summer Pudding Club gatherings. Don't be tempted to buy cheap chocolate; look for chocolate that has a high cocoa content and you will be well rewarded.

Serves 6

Cake

2 EGGS	50G (2 OZ) SELF-RAISING FLOUR,
50G (2 OZ) CASTER SUGAR	SIFTED

Filling

I LEVEL TBSP POWDERED GELATINE	425ML (I PINT) SINGLE CREAM
3 EGGS, SEPARATED	175G (6 OZ) PLAIN CHOCOLATE,
40G (I½ OZ) CASTER SUGAR	GRATED

Icing

110G (4 OZ) PLAIN CHOCOLATE	GRATED CHOCOLATE, TO
150ML (¼ PINT) DOUBLE CREAM	DECORATE
EXTRA CREAM, STRAWBERRIES AND	

Preheat the oven to 200°C/400°F/Gas 6.

To make the cake, whisk the eggs and sugar until they are thick and creamy. Stir in the sifted flour. Turn the mixture into a lightly greased 15 x 15cm (6 x 6 in) cake tin and bake in the oven for 12 minutes, or until springy to the touch. Turn out and cool.

Cut out a circle from the cake to fit into the bottom of 1.5 litre (2½ pint) pudding bowl. Cut the remaining cake into wedges to line the sides of the bowl.

To make the filling, put 3 tablespoons of water in a small basin or cup, sprinkle on the powdered gelatine and leave to soften. Meanwhile, whisk the egg yolks and sugar together until they are thick and creamy. Bring the single cream to a boil and whisk in the egg-yolk mixture. Stir in the gelatine until it has dissolved. Add the grated chocolate and stir until it has melted. Leave to cool, stirring occasionally.

Whisk the egg whites to form soft peaks rather than a dry, stiff mixture, and fold into the cooled chocolate mixture. Pour into the cake-lined bowl and leave to set, covered, for 4 hours, or overnight. Unmould the pudding on to a large plate.

For the icing, break the chocolate into small squares, put into a pan with the double cream and heat gently until the chocolate has melted, beating well. Remove from the heat and allow to cool slightly. Spoon over the bombe. Chill in the fridge until the icing has set. Decorate with swirls of cream, strawberries and grated chocolate.

Meringue Cake

Always popular, this cake can be filled with a variety of fruits, e.g. raspberries, chopped strawberries or nectarines. The addition of 50-75g (2-3 oz) of chopped walnuts or hazelnuts adds a nice crunch. A fruit sauce could also be served with it (see Vanilla Cream, page 19).

Serves 6-8

4 EGG WHITES	½ TSP WHITE VINEGAR
PINCH OF SALT	275ML (½ PINT) DOUBLE CREAM,
250G (9 OZ) CASTER SUGAR	WHIPPED
1 TSP VANILLA ESSENCE	ICING SUGAR, TO DECORATE

Preheat the oven to 190°C/375°F/Gas 5.

Line two 20cm (8 in) cake tins with lightly oiled greaseproof or parchment paper.

Whisk the egg whites with a pinch of salt until stiff. Beat in the sugar, a tablespoon at a time, followed by the vanilla essence and vinegar. Beat together until very stiff.

Divide the mixture between the two cake tins and spread out with a spatula. Bake in the oven for 40 minutes. Cool in the tins. Turn out and sandwich together with the whipped cream. Decorate with swirls of whipped cream and dust with icing sugar. Serve with a fruit sauce.

Variations

Stir 50-75g (2-3 oz) toasted and chopped hazelnuts or 50-75g (2-3 oz) chopped walnuts into the meringue mix.

Add raspberries, chopped strawberries or peaches to the filling.

Strawberry Galette

A quickly put-together dessert. Raspberries or sliced nectarines could be used instead of the strawberries. If you do use a different fruit, replace the strawberry jam with raspberry or apricot jam.

Serves 4-6

200G (7 OZ) PUFF PASTRY	GRATED RIND AND JUICE OF 1
275ML (½ PINT) DOUBLE CREAM	SMALL ORANGE
10G (½ OZ) CASTER SUGAR OR SOFT	350G (12 OZ) STRAWBERRIES
BROWN SUGAR	175G (6 OZ) STRAWBERRY JAM
2 TBSP GRAND MARNIER OR	
COINTREAU	

Preheat the oven to 220°C/425°F/Gas 7.

Grease a rectangular tin, 20 x 13cm (8 x 5 in). Roll the pastry out to a rectangle that is slightly larger than the tin and press into the tin. Press up the edges well, to make a border. Prick the base all over with a fork, then bake in the oven for 7-8 minutes. Remove from the oven and prick the base again. Bake for another 5 minutes until golden brown.

Whip the cream, then slowly beat in the sugar, liqueur and orange rind. Spread this mixture over the base of the cold pastry case. Arrange the strawberries on top.

Warm the jam and orange juice together in a small pan until the jam has melted. Sieve, then return to the pan and boil for 1-2 minutes. Remove from the heat and allow to cool, stirring occasionally. Spoon over the strawberries and leave to set.

Lime and Mint Cheesecake

A lovely, fresh-tasting and easy to make cheesecake. If you don't have a flan ring or flat, sideless baking tray, use a pretty 15cm (6 in) china dish instead.

Serves 6-8

Base

175G (6 OZ) DIGESTIVE BISCUITS, CRUSHED	PINCH OF GROUND MACE OR NUTMEG
75G (3 OZ) BUTTER, MELTED	

Filling

10G (½ OZ) GELATINE	150ML (¼ PINT) DOUBLE CREAM, WHIPPED
225G (8 OZ) CREAM CHEESE	
GRATED RIND AND JUICE OF 2 LIMES	65ML (2½ FL OZ) CRÈME FRAÎCHE
6 MINT LEAVES, CHOPPED	EXTRA WHIPPED CREAM AND MINT LEAVES, TO DECORATE
50G (2 OZ) CASTER SUGAR	

To make the biscuit base, place an oiled flan ring on a flat baking tray, or lightly oil a china dish. Mix together the biscuits, butter and spice and press out into the flan ring.

For the filling, put 2 tablespoons of water and the lime juice into a small bowl or cup, sprinkle on the gelatine and place in a pan of simmering water until the gelatine has dissolved and is clear.

Beat the cream cheese until soft and then add the remaining ingredients. Stir in the gelatine. Pile the mixture into the flan ring and allow to set.

Remove the cheesecake from the flan ring on to a serving plate. Decorate with swirls of whipped cream and mint leaves.

Spread a little melted chocolate on to the biscuit base.

Use crushed ginger biscuits for the base, but cut down a little on the melted butter.

Gooseberry Fool

You can make fools with a variety of fruits, but the tartness and texture of the gooseberry make it the perfect choice.

Serves 4

50G (2 OZ) UNSALTED BUTTER	75G (3 OZ) CASTER SUGAR
500G (1 LB) GOOSEBERRIES,	300ML (½ PINT) WHIPPING OR
TOPPED AND TAILED	DOUBLE CREAM

Melt the butter in a large pan and add the gooseberries and sugar. Stir and cook very gently, with a lid on, for 10-15 minutes, or until the fruit has softened but not disintegrated. Remove from the heat and crush the fruit with a potato masher. The end result should be a mash rather than a purée. Allow to cool.

Whip the cream until it just holds its shape and fold in the cooled fruit. Taste and add more sugar if needed. Serve with biscuits.

Charlotte Louisa

You will need a 450g (1 lb) loaf tin or small soufflé dish for this rich dessert. Some fresh raspberries or blackcurrants could be added to the mixture if you prefer.

Serves 6-8

50G (2 OZ) RAISINS	275ML (½ PINT) WHIPPING OR
2 TBSP RUM, BRANDY OR ORANGE	DOUBLE CREAM, PLUS EXTRA TO
LIQUEUR	DECORATE
1 PACKET (ABOUT 32 BISCUITS)	50G (2 OZ) FLAKED ALMONDS,
BOUDOIR BISCUITS	TOASTED, PLUS EXTRA TO
1 EGG WHITE, LIGHTLY WHISKED	DECORATE
175G (6 OZ) UNSALTED BUTTER,	50G (2 OZ) PLAIN CHOCOLATE,
SOFTENED	GRATED, PLUS EXTRA TO
175G (6 OZ) CASTER SUGAR	DECORATE

Soak the raisins in the liqueur and leave for a couple of hours.

Line the loaf tin or soufflé dish with clingfilm. Dip each biscuit in egg white and line the tin with them. Cream the butter and sugar until light and fluffy.

Whip the cream and stir into the butter mixture, together with the almonds, chocolate and raisins. Spoon into the biscuit-lined tin and trim the tops of the biscuits so that they are level with the top of the tin. Allow the pudding to set in the fridge for 2-3 hours.

Carefully run a palette knife between the clingfilm and the tin and turn out on to a serving dish. Decorate with swirls of whipped cream, grated chocolate and flaked, toasted almonds.

Almond and Raspberry Flan

Almond pastry, raspberries and an almond meringue combine to make this a particularly more-ish dessert.

Serves 4-6

Pastry

75G (3 OZ) BUTTER, DICED	50G (2 OZ) CASTER SUGAR
110G (4 OZ) PLAIN FLOUR	1 WHOLE EGG, BEATEN
50G (2 OZ) GROUND ALMONDS	A FEW DROPS OF VANILLA ESSENCE

Filling

2 EGG WHITES	110G (4 OZ) GROUND ALMONDS
110G (4 OZ) CASTER SUGAR	225G (8 OZ) FRESH RASPBERRIES

Preheat the oven to 180°C/350°F/Gas 4.

To make the pastry, rub the butter into the flour and ground almonds until the mixture resembles fine breadcrumbs. Stir in the sugar and then the beaten egg and vanilla essence. If the mixture is still a little crumbly, add a little more egg. Cover and leave the pastry to rest in fridge for 30 minutes.

Roll out the pastry and use it to line a 20cm (8 in) loose-bottomed cake tin or a similar-sized earthenware dish. Refrigerate again for 20-30 minutes. Remove the pastry base from the fridge and prick all over with a fork.

For the filling, beat the egg whites until stiff, then beat in the sugar, a little at a time, and fold in the almonds. Scatter the raspberries on the pastry base and spread the almond mixture on top. Bake the flan in the oven for 30-40 minutes, or until golden and set. Serve with a bowl of whipped cream.

Baked Cheesecake

Cheesecakes may be thought of as 'old hat', but they are still extremely popular. This is a particularly good recipe. By adding 50g (2 oz) of raisins soaked in 2 tablespoons of rum, you could turn it into a rum 'n' raisin cheesecake.

Serves 6-8

Base

12 PLAIN DIGESTIVE BISCUITS	75G (3 OZ) BUTTER, MELTED

Filling

225G (8 OZ) COTTAGE CHEESE	1 TSP VANILLA ESSENCE
225G (8 OZ) CREAM CHEESE	50G (2 OZ) BUTTER, MELTED
2 TBSP CASTER SUGAR	1½ TBSP CORNFLOUR
2 EGGS, BEATEN	1 TBSP PLAIN FLOUR
2 TBSP LEMON JUICE	250ML (9 FL OZ) DOUBLE CREAM

Preheat the oven to 180°C/350°F/Gas 4.

Make the base by crushing the biscuits into the melted butter. Mix well, then use to line the base of a 20cm (8 in) pie dish or flan ring.

If you have a food processor, put the cottage cheese in and whizz it up; otherwise, push it through a sieve.

Beat the two cheeses and the sugar together; this can be done in a processor or a mixer. Gradually add the beaten eggs, lemon juice and vanilla essence. Beat well. Stir in the melted butter, flours and cream. Beat again, then pour into the biscuit base and bake in the oven for about 1 hour. If the filling is not set after an hour,

Chocolate Bombe is a great favourite at
Summer Pudding Club gatherings.
See page 24.

 Meringue Cake can be filled with a variety of fruits
with nuts added for extra crunch.
See page 26.

A crisp base and succulent strawberries make
Strawberry Galette ideal for summer entertaining.
See page 27.

Lime and Mint Cheesecake is a fresh-tasting variation
on a classic dessert.
See page 28.

cover loosely with foil, turn down the heat to 170°C/325°F/Gas 3 and bake for a further 15-20 minutes, or until set. Allow to cool.

When cold you could make a topping of 55ml (2 fl oz) of soured cream mixed with 1 teaspoon of caster sugar.

Tipsy Strawberries

You don't have to include the variety or quantity of alcohol listed below, but it does make for wonderful eating!

Serves 4-6

450G (1 LB) FRESH STRAWBERRIES	1 TBSP KIRSCH
3 TBSP ICING SUGAR	275ML (½ PINT) DOUBLE CREAM
1 TBSP RUM	MINT LEAVES, TO DECORATE
2 TBSP COINTREAU	

Wash, drain and hull the strawberries; reserve a few for decoration. Cut the remainder in half if they are large. Put the strawberries in a bowl and scatter with 2 tablespoons of the icing sugar. Pour over the liqueurs, cover and chill for 1-2 hours.

Sieve the remaining icing sugar, whip the cream, add the sugar to the whipped cream and stir in the strawberries. Spoon the mixture into wine glasses or a pretty glass bowl. Cover and chill again for 1 hour. Decorate with whole fruit and mint leaves and serve with home-made biscuits.

You could also pile this mixture on to a biscuit base (see Baked Cheesecake, page 32).

CHAPTER THREE

Fresh and Fruity

THE PUDDINGS in this section are a tribute to the wonderful bounty of fresh soft fruits that this country can offer during the months of June and July – blackcurrants and redcurrants, straw-berries and raspberries, cherries and gooseberries. And we should not forget the humble rhubarb, which makes a great addition to almost any fruit dish because of its capacity to take on the flavour of other fruits. In this section, pride of place goes to the famous 'Summer Pudding', which has become a must at each meeting of the Summer Pudding Club. We could and did ring the changes on the other six puds, but this one just had to be on the list.

Summer Pudding

This classic English pudding has been around since the eighteenth century. There are now many variations of the recipe, but we are giving you the simplest and the best! You do need to start making it the day before you intend to eat it.

Serves 6-8

6–8 SLICES OF TWO-DAY-OLD BREAD, CUT INTO 1CM (½ IN) SLICES AND CRUSTS REMOVED	(STONED), GOOSEBERRIES, REDCURRANTS, WASHED AND HULLED (N.B. 110–175G (4–6
700G (1½ LB) SOFT FRUITS, E.G. RASPBERRIES, STRAWBERRIES, BLACKCURRANTS, CHERRIES	OZ) BLACKCURRANTS MUST BE INCLUDED IN THE MIX)
	110G (4 OZ) CASTER SUGAR

Cover the base of an 870ml (1½ pint) pudding bowl with 1 or 2 slices of bread. Line the sides of the bowl with more bread, fitting the slices closely together.

Wash the prepared fruit, put in a wide, heavy-based pan and sprinkle the sugar over the fruit. Bring to a simmer over a gentle heat and cook for 2–3 minutes, until the sugar melts and the juices from the fruit begin to run. Spoon the fruit and the juice into the prepared bowl. Reserve a few spoonfuls of juice for later use.

Make a lid for the pudding with the remaining bread. Put a plate large enough to fit inside the bowl on top of the pudding and weigh it down with 1 or 2 heavy tins. Put in the fridge for at least 8 hours.

To turn out, place a serving plate on top of the bowl and turn the whole lot upside-down to unmould the pudding. Use the reserved juices to patch up any parts of the bread that have not been soaked with juice. Serve with whipped cream.

If you don't have access to a variety of fresh soft fruits, supermarkets have an excellent mixture of summer fruits in their freezer section.

Variations

Use slices of brioche, crusts removed, instead of bread.

For an autumn pudding, use stewed apples and blackberries instead of the summer fruits.

Fresh Pineapple with Strawberries and Mango Cream

Serves 4

2 SMALL PINEAPPLES	HULLED AND WASHED
225G (8 OZ) STRAWBERRIES,	

Mango Cream

I RIPE MANGO, PEELED	RUNNY HONEY (OPTIONAL)
I 50ML (¼ PINT) DOUBLE CREAM,	
WHIPPED	

Cut the pineapples in half lengthways, making sure that each half has an equal number of green leaves. With a grapefruit knife, carefully remove the flesh, leaving the shells intact. Cut the flesh into cubes.

Halve the strawberries and mix with the pineapple cubes. Pile the fruit back into the pineapple shells.

For the mango cream, purée, process or blend the mango flesh and fold into the whipped cream. Add a little honey if you prefer it sweetened.

Fruit Salad served in Biscuit Containers

The fruit you use is entirely up to you, but it will look particularly attractive if you concentrate either on green fruits (grapes, kiwi, apple, melon, green-gages) or red (raspberries, strawberries, redcurrants, plums).

Serves 4

APPROX 700G (1½ LB) FRUIT	CASTER SUGAR, TO TASTE
A LITTLE ORANGE OR APPLE JUICE	
OR COINTREAU	

Prepare the fruit by washing and cutting it into an appropriate size. Sprinkle with the fruit juice or Cointreau and a little sugar. Leave for 1–2 hours so that the fruit can absorb the liqueur and sugar.

Pile the mixture into Biscuit Containers (see page 88) and serve with some whipped (or mango) cream (see page 36) as an accompaniment.

Butterscotch Apricots

Serves 4

16 APRICOTS	GROUND CINNAMON
25G (1 OZ) CASTER SUGAR	

Sauce

2 TBSP BRANDY	110G (4 OZ) UNSALTED BUTTER
2 TBSP DOUBLE CREAM	50G (2 OZ) DEMERARA SUGAR

Preheat the oven to 150°C/300°F/Gas 2.

Halve the apricots and remove the stones. Place them in a lightly buttered casserole dish (preferably in one layer), sprinkle the sugar and cinnamon over them, add 1–2 tablespoons of water and bake in the oven for 10-20 minutes. The cooking time will depend on the ripeness of the fruit; the apricots need to soften but still hold their shape.

Place all the sauce ingredients in a pan and heat until they have melted. Bring to a boil and allow the sauce to thicken slightly. The butterscotch sauce should be served warm rather than hot.

Green Fruit Salad

A very fresh-looking fruit salad, with the fruit soaked in lime juice and wine.

Serves 4-6

RIND AND JUICE OF 1 LIME	110G (4 OZ) SEEDLESS GREEN GRAPES
75G (3 OZ) CASTER SUGAR	1 GRAPEFRUIT
75ML (3 FL OZ) DRY WHITE WINE	2 KIWI FRUIT
1 SMALL OGEN OR ½ HONEYDEW	1 RIPE AVOCADO (OPTIONAL)
MELON	2 GREEN-SKINNED APPLES

Cut the rind from the lime, leaving the pith behind, and slice the rind into thin strips. Simmer in 150ml (¼ pint) of water for 5 minutes, then strain and reserve the cooking liquor. Make the liquor up to 150ml (¼ pint) again with more water and put in a pan with the sugar. Heat gently until the sugar has dissolved, then boil for 2-3 minutes to make a syrup. Add the wine and pour into a serving dish.

Cut the melon flesh into 2cm (1 in) cubes, or scoop it out with a melon baller. Add to the syrup.

Wash the grapes, leaving them whole, peel and slice the kiwi fruit and cut the grapefruit into segments. Add them all to the melon, plus any juice from the grapefruit. Chill.

About 2 hours before serving, dice the flesh of the avocado or scoop it out with a melon baller. Wash and quarter the apples and remove the cores. Slice thinly and toss the apple slices and the avocado flesh in the juice from the lime. Add to the salad. Sprinkle with the strips of lime peel, cover and chill until needed. Serve with home-made biscuits.

Summer Fruits
in Blackcurrant Jelly

Serves 4-6

225G (8 OZ) BLACKCURRANTS	225G (8 OZ) STRAWBERRIES
60G (2½ OZ) CASTER SUGAR	110G (4 OZ) RASPBERRIES
110G (4 OZ) CHERRIES, STONED WEIGHT	4 TSP POWDERED GELATINE

Bring the blackcurrants and 75ml (3 fl oz) of water to a boil, reduce the heat and simmer, covered, for 10 minutes. Remove from the heat and rub the fruit through a sieve. Pour the purée into a measuring jug and add enough cold water to make it up to 275ml (½ pint).

Return the purée to the pan and add the sugar. Stir over a gentle heat to dissolve the sugar, then bring to a boil. Remove from the heat and add the other fruits.

Meanwhile, pour 55ml (2 fl oz) of hot water into a small bowl or cup, sprinkle on the gelatine and leave for 2-3 minutes. Place the bowl in a pan of simmering water and stir until the gelatine becomes clear. Stir the gelatine into the fruit mixture. Pour into a rinsed-out 725ml (1¼ pint) bowl or ring mould and leave to set overnight.

Unmould on to a serving dish.

It looks wonderful if you decorate the jelly and/or the serving dish with strawberry or blackcurrant leaves and some small bunches of blackcurrants, whole raspberries and strawberries.

Blackberry Charlotte

Charlotte puddings originated in France. You could substitute the redcurrants, raspberries or blackcurrants for the blackberries.

Serves 6-8

110G (4 OZ) CASTER SUGAR	65ML (2½ FL OZ) DOUBLE OR
450G (1 LB) BLACKBERRIES	WHIPPING CREAM
2 LEVEL DSTSP CORNFLOUR	JUICE OF ½ LEMON
2 EGG YOLKS	110G (4 OZ) SPONGE FINGERS

Meringue Topping

2 EGG WHITES	65ML (2½ FL OZ) BLACKBERRY
110G (4 OZ) ICING SUGAR	SYRUP

Preheat the oven to 150°C/300°F/Gas 2.

Put the sugar and 275ml (½ pint) of water in a pan and heat gently until the sugar has dissolved. Add the blackberries and cook on a low heat for 10 minutes. Strain and reserve the syrup and put the blackberries to one side.

Put the cornflour in a small pan and gradually blend in 275ml (½ pint) of the blackberry syrup. Cook for a few minutes, stirring all the time. Remove from the heat.

Beat the egg yolks and cream into the blackberry mixture. Add the lemon juice and more sugar, if needed.

Cut off one rounded end of each of the sponge fingers. Pour enough of the blackberry cream into a 570ml (1 pint) soufflé dish to cover the bottom, then stand the sponge fingers, cut side down, around the inside of the dish. Put a layer of blackberries over the cream, followed by another layer of cream, and so on until all the berries and cream have been used up.

For the meringue topping, put the egg whites into a bowl with the icing sugar and the remaining blackberry syrup and whisk over a pan of boiling water until the meringue stands in soft peaks. Remove the bowl from the heat and keep whisking until the meringue has cooled.

Pile or pipe the meringue on to the charlotte.

Bake in the oven for 20 minutes. Serve cold with whipped cream.

Victoria Plums in Tawny Port

The port can be replaced by Madeira wine, if preferred.

Serves 6-8

700-900G (1½-2 LB) VICTORIA PLUMS	I TSP GROUND CINNAMON (OR I STICK)
75G (3 OZ) SOFT BROWN SUGAR	2 TBSP FLAKED ALMONDS,
275ML (½ PINT) TAWNY PORT	TOASTED, TO DECORATE
JUICE OF I ORANGE	(OPTIONAL)

Remove the stalks from the plums and wash.

Dissolve the sugar in 275ml (½ pint) of water and boil for 10 minutes. Remove from the heat, stir in the port, orange juice and cinnamon and bring back to a simmer. Add the fruit to the hot syrup, cover with a lid and remove from the heat. Leave the plums in the syrup for 15-20 minutes.

Lift the fruit out with a perforated spoon and put into a serving dish. Return the syrup to the heat and boil until it has reduced by one-third and thickened slightly. Remove the cinnamon stick, if used, and pour the hot syrup over the plums.

This pudding is best served warm. Scatter the almonds over just before serving, and hand round home-made biscuits as an accompaniment.

Red Fruit Salad

Use a combination of whatever soft red fruits are available: strawberries, cherries, loganberries, redcurrants, blackberries, raspberries and blackcurrants all work well.

Serves 4

450G (1 LB) MIXED RED FRUITS	75-110G (3-4 OZ) GRANULATED
RIND AND JUICE OF 1 ORANGE	SUGAR
1 TBSP REDCURRANT JELLY	

Hull and wash the fruit. Stone the cherries, if using.

Take a few large strips of the orange rind, avoiding the pith, and put this in a pan, together with the juice, jelly, 125ml (4 fl oz) of water and sugar. Heat gently until the sugar has dissolved, boil the liquid for 3-4 minutes to make a syrup, then sieve it. If using cherries, redcurrants or blackcurrants, add them now to the hot syrup. Leave to cool before adding the remaining fruit. Cover and chill. Serve with home-made biscuits.

Fresh Apricot and Brandy Trifle

A fresh-tasting and rich trifle. If you prefer, replace the Amaretti biscuits with trifle sponge.

Serves 4-6

450G (1 LB) FRESH APRICOTS	570ML (1 PINT) CUSTARD
50G (2 OZ) CASTER SUGAR	150ML (¼ PINT) DOUBLE CREAM
75ML (3 FL OZ) BRANDY	TOASTED ALMONDS AND EXTRA
225G (8 OZ) AMARETTI BISCUITS,	APRICOTS, TO DECORATE
ROUGHLY CRUSHED	

Wash the apricots, cut them in half and remove the stones. Put 150ml (¼ pint) of water in a pan, add the sugar and heat gently until the sugar has dissolved. Add the apricots and poach gently in the syrup until they have softened (about 10 minutes). Remove from the heat and lift the apricots out with a perforated spoon.

When the fruit has cooled a little, put it into a serving dish and pour over the apricot syrup and brandy. Sprinkle the crushed Amaretti biscuits over the fruit and gently stir in. Spoon the custard over, cover the dish and chill for 2 hours.

Whip the cream and spread over the trifle. Decorate with toasted almonds and sliced apricots.

CHAPTER FOUR

Children's
Favourites

IT IS AN EXTRAORDINARY phenomenon that we adults pretend that many of the best experiences in life are not for our benefit but for our children. Yet we secretly adore them, and in many cases enjoy them much more than the youngsters do. For example, who gets the most fun out of model railways or Winnie-the-Pooh? The grown-ups of course! Nevertheless, for some reason we are reluctant to admit it. It is the same with so-called children's party fare; here are a few recipes which are as much a treat for adults as for the children.

Choc and Marshmallow Tart

As children would say, this is really wicked!

Serves 4-6

Base

175G (6 OZ) CHOCOLATE DIGESTIVE BISCUITS	75G (3 OZ) BUTTER, MELTED

Filling

1 TSP GELATINE	275ML (½ PINT) DOUBLE CREAM, WHIPPED
55ML (2 FL OZ) MILK	
110G (4 OZ) BAG OR POT MARSH-MALLOWS	GRATED CHOCOLATE, TO DECORATE

To make the base, crush the biscuits finely and mix with the melted butter. Lightly oil a 20cm (8 in) flan tin and press the biscuit mixture into the bottom. Refrigerate.

For the filling, sprinkle the gelatine over the milk and allow to soak for 10 minutes. Put the gelatine mixture and the marshmallows in a pan and stir over a low heat until the marshmallows have melted. Do not let them boil. Remove from the heat and allow to cool.

Fold in the whipped cream and pour over the biscuit base. Sprinkle with grated chocolate and refrigerate for 2-3 hours.

Butterscotch Yoghurt Ice-cream

Children will love the rich taste of butterscotch combined with thick yoghurt and served in the form of an ice-cream.

Serves 6-8

55ML (2 FL OZ) EVAPORATED MILK OR WHIPPING CREAM	40G (1½ OZ) BROWN SUGAR
	1 TSP VANILLA ESSENCE
1 TSP GELATINE	570ML (1 PINT) THICK GREEK
75G (3 OZ) BUTTER	YOGHURT
PINCH OF SALT	

Put 1 tablespoon of the evaporated milk or cream in a small bowl or cup and sprinkle on the gelatine. Leave to soak for at least 5 minutes.

Melt the butter in a pan, add the salt and sugar and stir over a low heat until the sugar has dissolved. Add the remaining evaporated milk or cream, gelatine mixture and vanilla essence. Heat through until everything has dissolved. Allow the mixture to cool until it is lukewarm. Stir the yoghurt into the butterscotch mixture.

Turn into a plastic container and freeze for about an hour. Beat the mixture to break up any ice crystals. Repeat this process a further two or three times. The ice-cream can be served straight from the freezer.

Orange and Pineapple Jelly

Jellies are always popular. This one looks stunning if made in a ring mould. It has the added bonus of being a very healthy sweet, too.

Serves 6-8

570ML (1 PINT) FRESH ORANGE JUICE	290G (10½ OZ) TIN MANDARIN ORANGES (OR FRESH)
4 LEVEL TSP GELATINE	
400G (14 OZ) TIN PINEAPPLE CHUNKS (OR FRESH)	

Put 3 tablespoons of orange juice in a small bowl or cup and sprinkle on the gelatine. Leave to soak for 10 minutes. Stand the bowl in a pan of simmering water, stirring occasionally, until the gelatine has dissolved and looks clear. Stir the gelatine mixture into the remaining orange juice, then add half of the drained pineapple chunks and mandarins. Pour into a 1.2 litre (2 pint) ring mould, jelly mould or bowl and refrigerate for 2-3 hours until set.

Unmould the jelly and fill the centre of the ring with the remaining fruit, or arrange the fruit around the outside of the jelly.

Strawberry Sherbet

This is really simple to make and will please adults and children alike. Serve with a bowl of fresh strawberries.

Serves 6-8

APPROX. 450G (1 LB) STRAWBERRIES, ENOUGH TO MAKE 275ML (½ PINT) JUICE	225G (8 OZ) GRANULATED SUGAR JUICE OF 1½ LEMONS

Blend or liquidize the strawberries, then push them through a sieve.

Place the sugar in a pan with 275ml (½ pint) of the water. Stir over a low heat until the sugar has dissolved. Bring to a boil, without stirring, and allow to boil for 2-3 minutes. Remove the syrup from the heat and allow to go cold. Pour into a bowl and add the strawberry juice, lemon juice and 570ml (1 pint) of water. Pour into a plastic container, cover and freeze until set, about 3 hours.

Remove the sherbet from the freezer. Blend or liquidize until it is smooth, then return it to the container. Cover and freeze again until it is set.

Choc Cream Pie

Serves 6-8

Base

225G (8 OZ) DIGESTIVE BISCUITS	110G (4 OZ) BUTTER, MELTED

Filling

275ML (½ PINT) MILK	25G (1 OZ) UNSALTED BUTTER
25G (1 OZ) CASTER SUGAR	75G (3 OZ) PLAIN CHOCOLATE,
1½ TSP CORNFLOUR	GRATED
25G (1 OZ) PLAIN FLOUR	ICING SUGAR
2 EGGS	

Topping

150ML (¼ PINT) DOUBLE CREAM	GRATED CHOCOLATE, TO DECORATE

To make the base, crush the biscuits into fine crumbs and mix with the melted butter. Spread the mixture into the base and up the sides of a 20cm (8 in) flan dish. Chill in the fridge for 2 hours.

For the filling, heat the milk in a pan. Meanwhile, combine the sugar, flours and eggs in a bowl and beat well. Gradually beat in the warm milk. Return the mixture to the pan and cook over a low heat, stirring until it thickens and just about comes to the boil. Remove from the heat and stir in the butter and chocolate. Allow to cool slightly. Spoon the mixture into the biscuit base, level out and dust with icing sugar, to prevent a skin forming. Chill.

Before serving, whip the cream and spread it over the pie, decorating it with the grated chocolate.

Chocolate Nut Slice

A delicious mixture of chocolate, nuts and cherries made into the form of a loaf.

Serves 6-8

75G (3 OZ) PLAIN CHOCOLATE	75G (3 OZ) GLACÉ CHERRIES,
75G (3 OZ) UNSALTED BUTTER	ROUGHLY CHOPPED
4 TBSP GOLDEN SYRUP	75G (3 OZ) ALMONDS, TOASTED, OR
350G (12 OZ) PLAIN DIGESTIVES OR	BROKEN WALNUTS
CHOCOLATE DIGESTIVES,	
ROUGHLY BROKEN	

Line a 450g (1 lb) loaf tin with clingfilm.

In a pan, melt the chocolate, broken up roughly, with the butter and syrup, stirring all the time. Remove from the heat, add the biscuits, cherries and nuts, and mix well. Press the mixture into the loaf tin and allow to cool. It is ready when it has set hard. Serve in thin slices with a bowl of whipped cream or ice-cream.

Note

For ease of measuring out the syrup, dip the spoon in boiling water first and the syrup will slip off the spoon quite easily.

Blancmange

This is the traditional vanilla blancmange. If you don't have a jelly mould, just use a regular bowl-shaped basin.

Serves 6-8

75G (3 OZ) CORNFLOUR	50G (2 OZ) CASTER SUGAR
I LITRE (1¾ PINTS) CREAMY MILK	A LITTLE VANILLA ESSENCE

Blend the cornflour with a little of the milk and bring the remaining milk to a boil. Pour the boiling milk on to the cornflour mixture, stirring all the time. Return the mixture to the heat and bring back to the boil, stirring continuously. Simmer very slowly for 5 minutes, stirring occasionally. Remove from the heat and stir in the sugar and vanilla essence to taste.

Pour the blancmange into a wetted jelly mould or bowl. Cover and leave to cool. Chill for at least 2 hours, then unmould to serve.

Variations

For chocolate blancmange, add cocoa to the cornflour mixture. Or stir 175g (6 oz) of plain chocolate, broken into pieces, into the hot milk mixture.

For strawberry blancmange, replace 275ml (½ pint) of milk with a strawberry purée, adding this to the cornflour mixture before pouring on the hot milk.

Quick Creamy Jelly

Serves 4

1 X 125G (4½ OZ) ORANGE- OR STRAWBERRY-FLAVOURED JELLY	2 TBSP CUSTARD POWDER
	225ML (8 FL OZ) MILK
3 TBSP ORANGE JUICE OR RIBENA	125ML (4 FL OZ) DOUBLE CREAM

Heat 100ml (3½ fl oz) of water and add the cubes of jelly. Stir until the cubes have dissolved, then add the orange juice or Ribena. Leave to cool.

In a bowl, blend the custard powder with a little of the milk. Bring the rest of the milk to a boil, then pour it slowly on to the custard mixture. Pour the custard into a clean pan and bring it back to the boil, stirring all the time, until it thickens.

Allow the custard to cool slightly, then stir it into the jelly. Cool until nearly set.

Lightly whip the cream and fold into the setting jelly mix. Pour into 4 glasses and refrigerate for 1 hour until set.

Banana Trifle

We all love a trifle. This is a children's version, with no alcohol in it.

Serves 6-8

4 SLICES SPONGE CAKE, OR 12 SPONGE FINGERS	150ML (¼ PINT) DOUBLE CREAM, WHIPPED
3 TBSP RASPBERRY JAM	HUNDREDS AND THOUSANDS, TO DECORATE
4 SMALL BANANAS, THINLY SLICED	
275ML (½ PINT) WARM CUSTARD, FLAVOURED WITH A LITTLE VANILLA ESSENCE	

Roughly break up the sponge cake or fingers and lay them in a serving bowl. Spread the jam over them and top with the bananas. Pour over the warm vanilla custard.

Chill the trifle and then spread the whipped cream over the top. Sprinkle on hundreds and thousands.

Strawberry Fritters

These are gorgeous; the strawberries can be replaced by gooseberries, if topped and tailed, or equally well by blackcurrants or fresh apricot halves.

Makes 4-6

50G (2 OZ) PLAIN FLOUR	3 TBSP MILK
I TBSP CASTER SUGAR, PLUS EXTRA TO DECORATE	OIL, FOR DEEP-FAT FRYING
2 EGGS, SEPARATED	400G (14 OZ) STRAWBERRIES, HULLED

For the batter, stir the flour and sugar together, add the egg yolks and milk and beat until smooth. Whisk the egg whites until stiff, then fold them into the batter.

The oil for frying should be at least 7.5cm (3 in) deep. Heat the oil to 185°F/360°C, or until a cube of bread turns golden in 45 seconds.

Add the strawberries to the batter. Dip a perforated metal spoon into the hot fat, then use it to lift out two or three strawberries from the batter. Don't try to separate the strawberries. Carefully drop a spoonful of strawberries into the hot fat. Cook them in batches, six to nine at a time. Fry them until they are golden brown, turning once. Drain them on kitchen paper, sprinkle with caster sugar and serve at once with custard or cream.

CHAPTER FIVE

Puddings to Impress

I N T H I S C A T E G O R Y we have put the sort of desserts that will elicit from your family, friends or guests a response which is far in excess of the skill and effort employed in the making of them. Whether your guests are impressed by the appearance or by the flavour of the dessert, you will have the satisfaction of seeing them do a double-take as they first encounter these creations. Each one is a conversation-stopper.

Passionfruit Syllabub

The intense, scented flavour of passionfruit, combined with lemon and cream, makes a deliciously simple and elegant dessert. Serve with home-made crisp biscuits.

Serves 4-6

10 PASSIONFRUITS	275ML (½ PINT) WHIPPING OR
2 TBSP LEMON JUICE, PLUS SOME	DOUBLE CREAM, LIGHTLY
GRATED RIND TO DECORATE	WHIPPED
50–75G (2–3 OZ) ICING SUGAR,	2 EGG WHITES
SIFTED	

Cut the fruit in half and spoon out the flesh into a pan. Heat gently. Push the warmed fruit through a sieve into a bowl, reserving some of the seeds for decoration. Add the lemon juice to the passionfruit pulp, stir in the icing sugar and fold in the whipped cream. Beat the egg whites until they are stiff but not dry, then carefully fold them into the cream mixture. Spoon the syllabub into glasses, cover and refrigerate.

Serve the syllabub sprinkled with passionfruit seeds and a little grated lemon rind.

Chocolate Marquis

So simple, but divine. This chocolate dessert can be served on its own, or with a bowl of fresh raspberries or strawberries as an accompaniment.

Serves 6

75G (3 OZ) GOOD QUALITY PLAIN CHOCOLATE, GRATED	200G (7 OZ) UNSALTED BUTTER, DICED
50G (2 OZ) GOOD QUALITY WHITE CHOCOLATE, GRATED	6 EGGS, SEPARATED

Put the grated chocolate in a bowl over a pan of simmering water. Stir occasionally until the chocolate has melted. Beat in the butter, about 25g (1 oz) at a time, then add the egg yolks, one at a time, beating continuously. Remove the bowl from the heat. Whisk the egg whites until stiff but not dry, and fold into the chocolate mixture. Pour into a glass bowl, or individual dishes, and chill thoroughly.

Candied Fruit Ice-cream

A very impressive ice-cream bombe; it takes very little assembling but will earn lots of praise. You could line a mould first with vanilla ice-cream and, when you refreeze it, add a layer of chocolate or strawberry ice-cream to make it look even more impressive.

Serves 8

575G (1¼ LB) GOOD QUALITY VANILLA ICE-CREAM	150ML (¼ PINT) DOUBLE CREAM
110G (4 OZ) CANDIED FRUIT, CHOPPED	1 EGG WHITE
2 TBSP ORANGE LIQUEUR	EXTRA CANDIED FRUIT AND GRATED CHOCOLATE, TO DECORATE

Put the vanilla ice-cream in the fridge 30 minutes before you need it.

Place a 900g (2 lb) bowl or basin-shaped mould, preferably metal, in the freezer to get really cold. Mix the candied fruit and the liqueur together and set aside.

Using a spoon, spread the ice-cream over the inside of the bowl to make a thick wall. To help spread the ice-cream evenly, dip the spoon into ice-cold water first. Put the bowl back in the freezer. Whip the cream and whisk the egg white until stiff. Drain and dry the candied fruit, then fold in the egg white and cream. Pour this mixture into the vanilla ice-cream mould and refreeze for a minimum of 3 hours.

To turn out, dip the mould into hot water very briefly and invert on to a serving dish. Sprinkle with extra candied fruit and grated chocolate.

Raspberry Strudel

Simple, but different. You could use other soft fruit, such as apricots, black-berries, redcurrants or even a bag of defrosted mixed summer fruits.

Serves 6-8

1 TBSP ICING SUGAR	575G (1¼ LB) RASPBERRIES
225G (8 OZ) FILO PASTRY	50-75 (2-3 OZ) CASTOR SUGAR
110G (4 OZ) GROUND HAZELNUTS,	EXTRA ICING SUGAR, SIFTED, TO
TOASTED	DECORATE

Preheat the oven to 200°C/400°F/Gas 6.

Heat 55ml (2 fl oz) of water in a small pan. Add the icing sugar and stir until it has dissolved.

Layer up the sheets of filo pastry, brushing each layer with the sugared water. Sprinkle the pastry with hazelnuts, raspberries and sugar. Fold in the long edges of the pastry and roll up from the short end. Place, seam side down, on a baking tray and bake in the oven for 25-30 minutes. Serve warm, sprinkled with sifted icing sugar, and with a bowl of whipped cream to accompany it.

Peach Brûlée

A quick and delicious dessert. You can use other soft fruit instead of the peaches, e.g. grapes, orange segments or apple purée.

Serves 4

4 PEACHES, SKINNED	2 TBSP COINTREAU, OR OTHER
150ML (¼ PINT) DOUBLE CREAM	FRUIT LIQUEUR
75ML (3 FL OZ) THICK GREEK	75G (3 OZ) DEMERARA SUGAR
YOGHURT	

Quarter the peaches and place in four ramekin dishes, or one large, heat-resistant dish. Whip the double cream and fold in the yoghurt. Pour Cointreau over the fruit and then spread with the cream mixture. Sprinkle the sugar over in a thick layer.

Preheat a grill until it is really hot. Grill the brûlées for 3 minutes, or until the sugar has caramelized.

Lemon Cotswold

This lemon and cream cheese mixture is similar to the filling of a light cheese-cake. It can be served in glasses or in a biscuit crust.

Serves 4-6

275ML (½ PINT) LEMON JELLY TABLET	GRATED RIND OF I LEMON
	50G (2 OZ) CASTER SUGAR
225G (8 OZ) CREAM CHEESE	

Topping (optional)

3 TBSP LEMON JUICE	25G (I OZ) CASTER SUGAR
I ½ LEVEL TSP ARROWROOT	KNOB OF UNSALTED BUTTER

Put the jelly cubes in a measuring jug and add 300ml (½ pint) of boiling water. Stir until the cubes have dissolved and allow to cool in the fridge until it is on the point of setting, but not quite set solid.

Beat together the cream cheese, lemon rind and sugar, and gradually beat in the jelly. Pour this mixture into individual glasses and allow to set.

To make the topping, top up the lemon juice with water until it makes 150ml (¼ pint). Stir a little of this liquid into the arrowroot, mix to a paste and then add the rest of the liquid and the sugar. Transfer the mixture to a small pan and bring to a boil, stirring. Cook until the liquid is clear.

Remove from the heat and stir in the butter. Allow to cool a little and then pour over the Lemon Cotswold. Refrigerate until set. If you don't want to make this topping, decorate the pudding with whipped cream and perhaps some toasted almonds.

Chocolate and Ginger Nut Slice

If you're not a lover of ginger, use digestive or ratafia biscuits instead for this refrigerator cake.

Serves 4-6

110G (4 OZ) GOOD QUALITY PLAIN CHOCOLATE	50G (2 OZ) TOASTED ALMONDS, HAZELNUTS OR WALNUTS, CHOPPED
50G (2 OZ) UNSALTED BUTTER, MELTED	25G (1 OZ) CRYSTALLIZED GINGER, CHOPPED (OPTIONAL)
1 EGG, BEATEN	1 TBSP BRANDY OR ORANGE JUICE
75G (3 OZ) GINGER BISCUITS, CRUSHED	ICING SUGAR, TO DECORATE

Melt the chocolate in a bowl over a pan of simmering water. Remove from the heat and beat in the butter and egg. Stir the biscuits, nuts, ginger and brandy or orange juice into the chocolate mixture. Press it into a flan dish, or a 450g (1 lb) loaf tin lined with clingfilm. Chill for an hour or so. Serve sprinkled with icing sugar and a bowl of whipped cream. This pudding is also delicious with Mango Cream, (see page 36).

Butterscotch Pie

The base of this pie can be a regular shortcrust, a press-in shortcrust (see page 66) or a biscuit base. The rich butterscotch filling contrasts with the sharp topping of yoghurt and cream.

Serves 4-6

PASTRY TO LINE A 20CM (8 IN) LOOSE-BOTTOMED OR OVEN-PROOF FLAN TIN	75G (3 OZ) SOFT DARK BROWN SUGAR
2 LEVEL TBSP CORNFLOUR	150ML (¼ PINT) DOUBLE CREAM
410ML (14½ FL OZ) EVAPORATED MILK	150ML (¼ PINT) THICK GREEK YOGHURT
4 EGG YOLKS	A LITTLE DEMERARA SUGAR, TO DECORATE
75G (3 OZ) UNSALTED BUTTER	

Preheat the oven to 190°C/375°F/Gas 5.

Bake the pastry case blind: prick it all over with a fork, cover the base with foil and a layer of dried beans, then bake in the oven for 15 minutes. Remove the beans and foil and bake for a further 5 minutes.

In a bowl, mix the cornflour to a paste with a little of the evaporated milk. Put the egg yolks, butter and sugar into a pan with the remaining milk and bring to a simmer, stirring occasionally. Pour in the cornflour mixture and beat well, over the heat, for a few minutes, until bubbling and thick. Pour the filling into the pastry case. Cool, cover and leave until cold.

Whip the cream and fold in the yoghurt. Spoon this mixture on to the pie and sprinkle with demerara sugar.

Fruit has been piled into a scooped out pineapple for
Fresh Pineapple and Strawberries with Mango Cream.
See page 36.

Fruit Salad served in Biscuit Containers adds novelty
to a summer classic.
See page 37.

A meringue topping adds a luxurious touch
to Blackberry Charlotte.
See page 41.

 Victoria Plums in Tawny Port which has been spiced with cinnamon and orange make an easy but delicious dessert.
See page 42.

Fruit Salad looks especially appetising when made with
rich red soft fruits or fresh green ingredients
with a dash of white wine. See pages 43 and 39.

The combination of fresh fruit, almondy Amaretti biscuits and brandy make a fresh-tasting and rich Fresh Apricot and Brandy Trifle. See page 44.

This traditional Strawberry Blancmange is a perennial
children's favourite.
See page 52.

 Home-made Vanilla Ice Cream can be flavoured with chocolate and mint, banana and walnut, honey and whisky or toffee. See pages 69-70.

Raspberry and Ratafia Terrine

An elegant but simply put-together dessert.

Serves 4-6

4 LEVEL TSP GELATINE	16 RATAFIA BISCUITS, ROUGHLY
225G (8 OZ) RASPBERRIES, PLUS A	BROKEN
FEW TO DECORATE	A LITTLE HONEY OR CASTER SUGAR
2 TBSP CRÈME DE CASSIS OR	(OPTIONAL)
ORANGE LIQUEUR	MINT LEAVES, TO DECORATE
275ML (½ PINT) DOUBLE CREAM	

Raspberry Sauce

225G (8 OZ) RASPBERRIES	ICING SUGAR, TO TASTE
2 TBSP ORANGE JUICE	

Line a 450g (1 lb) loaf tin with clingfilm. Put 2 tablespoons of water in a cup and sprinkle on the gelatine. Leave it for 5 minutes, then place the cup in a small pan of simmering water and leave until the gelatine is clear. Allow it to cool for a few minutes.

Put the raspberries and the crème de Cassis in a food processor or liquidizer and blend until smooth. Alternatively, push the fruit through a sieve. Mix the fruit purée with the gelatine and cream, then fold in the roughly broken ratafias. Taste, and add a little honey or caster sugar, if needed. Pour the mixture into the loaf tin, cover and refrigerate until set (3-4 hours).

To make the sauce, blend all the sauce ingredients in a food processor, or push through a sieve, until you have a smooth liquid.

Turn out the terrine and pour over a little sauce. Decorate with a few whole fruit and mint leaves, and serve with raspberry sauce, chocolate sauce or cream.

The raspberries can be replaced by strawberries or blackberries.

Apple and Blackberry Tart

It is a good idea to have a quantity of this press-in shortcrust pastry mixture in the freezer for emergency entertaining. Simply freeze it at the fine breadcrumb stage. With its wonderfully light crust, this quickly put-together tart will always score top marks.

Serves 4-6

Pastry

175G (6 OZ) PLAIN FLOUR	3 TBSP CASTER SUGAR
PINCH OF SALT	75G (3 OZ) BUTTER, DICED
¼ TSP BAKING POWDER	I EGG, BEATEN

Filling

I EGG, SEPARATED	225G (8 OZ) BLACKBERRIES
50G (2 OZ) UNSALTED BUTTER, MELTED	450G (I LB) COOKING APPLES, PEELED, CORED AND SLICED
50G (2 OZ) SOFT LIGHT BROWN SUGAR, OR CASTER SUGAR	150ML (¼ PINT) DOUBLE CREAM, WHIPPED
½ TSP GROUND CINNAMON	

To make the pastry, combine the flour, salt, baking powder and sugar in a food processor or bowl. Add the diced butter and process until the mixture resembles fine breadcrumbs. If you don't have a food processor, rub the mixture by hand.

Tip the mixture into a bowl and add the beaten egg, mixing thoroughly with a knife. Press the crumbly dough into the bottom and around the sides of a 20cm (8 in) tart tin, preferably one with a loose bottom. Chill for 30 minutes before using.

Preheat the oven to 200°C/400°F/Gas 6.

To make the filling, beat the egg yolk into the cooled, melted butter, then add the sugar, cinnamon and blackberries, tossing them together until well mixed. Put the prepared apples into the pastry case and top with the blackberry mixture.

Bake in the oven for 30-40 minutes. Allow to cool.

Whisk the egg white until stiff and fold into the whipped cream. Pile on top of the tart just before serving.

CHAPTER SIX

Ice-creams and Sorbets

IT WAS Marco Polo who brought back from the East the secret of how to cool food without using ice or snow – thereby giving Italians their fine reputation as ice-cream makers. But it was in England, in about 1650, that milk, cream and eggs were first used in the production of ice-cream. (It is these ingredients that distinguished ice-creams from sorbets.) This development has been attributed to the chef of King Charles I. The word 'sorbet' is in fact derived from the same word as 'sherbet', although in this country sherbet is reserved for fruit juices, or extracts that are effervescent.

Vanilla Ice-cream

Serves 6-8

2 EGG YOLKS	275ML (½ PINT) MILK
I EGG	275ML (½ PINT) DOUBLE CREAM
2 TBSP CASTER OR ICING SUGAR	I TSP VANILLA ESSENCE, TO TASTE

Beat together the egg yolks and the whole egg. You can do this in a mixer or a blender. When the mixture is pale in colour, whisk in the sugar. Bring the milk and cream to a boil and gradually add to the egg mixture. Stir in vanilla essence to taste. Allow to cool, stirring from time to time.

If you have an ice-cream maker, pour in the mixture and churn for 20-30 minutes. Alternatively, pour into a plastic container and freeze in the coldest part of the freezer, then stir two or three times, at 1½-hour intervals.

Move the ice-cream to the fridge 30 minutes before you want to serve it.

Variations on basic Vanilla Ice-cream recipe

Banana and Walnut (or Pecan)

Add 225g (8 oz) of peeled and chopped banana, tossed in a little lemon juice, and 75g (3 oz) of chopped nuts to the warm ice-cream mixture.

Orange

Add a 350g (12 oz) jar of good quality marmalade and 2 table-spoons of orange liqueur.

Chocolate and Mint

Add 175g (6 oz) of good quality grated chocolate to the hot milk and stir, off the heat, until it has melted. When the mixture has cooled, stir in a handful of chopped mint leaves.

Honey and Whisky

Mix a 350g (12 oz) jar of clear honey with the eggs and beat together. Add the whisky just before putting the ice-cream into the freezer – the amount of whisky you add is up to you! A guideline would be 2-4 tablespoons.

Toffee

Simply boil a can of condensed milk for 3 hours, making sure the can is completely immersed in boiling water for the whole of the 3 hours. Empty the contents into the warm ice-cream mixture and whisk slowly until everything is well blended.

Fool's Ice-cream

So named, I believe, because any fool can make this soft-scoop version of vanilla ice-cream! Even better, you don't need to take it out of the freezer to stir it, either.

Serves 6-8

4 EGGS, SEPARATED	425ML (1 PINT) WHIPPING CREAM
110G (4 OZ) CASTER SUGAR	A FEW DROPS OF VANILLA ESSENCE

Beat together the egg yolks and the sugar until pale and fluffy. In separate bowls, beat the egg whites until they form soft peaks and whip the cream until it holds its shape. Gently stir the cream, vanilla essence and meringue into the egg yolk mixture until well blended. Pour into a plastic container, cover with a lid and freeze for 5-6 hours before it is needed.

Soft Fruit Ice-cream

You can make this ice-cream from raspberries, blackcurrants, redcurrants, gooseberries (or a combination of these). If using peaches, cherries or apricots, they should be stoned before you weigh them.

If you have an appropriate orange liqueur to add, it will certainly lift the flavour; gin also works well!

Serves 4-6

450G (1 LB) PREPARED FRUIT, SKINS REMOVED IF USING PEACHES OR APRICOTS	275ML (½ PINT) DOUBLE CREAM
THINLY CUT ZEST AND JUICE OF 1 ORANGE	150ML (¼ PINT) SINGLE CREAM
	ORANGE OR LEMON JUICE (OPTIONAL)
110G (4 OZ) ICING SUGAR, PLUS AN EXTRA 2 TBSP	2 EGG WHITES, STIFFLY BEATEN
	3 TBSP LIQUEUR OR GIN

Liquidize the fruit with the orange zest, juice and the 110g (4 oz) of icing sugar.

Whip the creams together with the 2 tablespoons of icing sugar until stiff, then fold in the fruit. Taste and adjust the sugar.

Freeze at the lowest temperature, or in an ice-cream maker.

When the mixture is almost frozen, but still slightly liquid in the centre, stir in the stiffly beaten egg whites. Be careful not to overwhip at this stage, or the ice-cream will melt too much. Flavour with the alcohol, then freeze again.

Transfer the ice-cream to the fridge 30 minutes before serving.

Note

If using raspberries or gooseberries, it is a good idea to sieve them after liquidizing, to remove the seeds.

Sauces to Serve with Ice-creams

Plum

Makes 3/4 pint

700G (1½ LB) PLUMS	A LITTLE PORT, GIN OR KIRSCH
225G (8 OZ) GRANULATED SUGAR	(OPTIONAL)

Put a thin layer of water in the base of a wide-bottomed pan. Slice the plums into it and cook gently until they are just soft. Purée the fruit in a blender or processor and sieve.

In a separate pan, dissolve the sugar in 4-5 tablespoons of water over a low heat, stirring continuously. When the sugar has dissolved, stop stirring, raise the heat and boil until the liquid becomes golden brown. Remove from the heat and stir in 6 tablespoons of water, taking care, as the caramel will spit. Put the pan back on a gentle heat, to get rid of any lumpiness. Add the plum purée and mix well. Cool a little before adding the alcohol.

Variations

Replace the plums with apricots, peaches or cherries.

Chocolate

Makes 1/2 pint

Gently melt 110g (4 oz) of good quality plain chocolate. Do this in a bowl over gently simmering water (but don't allow the bowl to come into contact with the water, or the chocolate may go lumpy and grainy). Off the heat, beat in the contents of a small tin of evaporated milk.

Raspberry or Strawberry

Makes 3/4 pint

450G (1 LB) FRUIT	A FEW DROPS OF LEMON JUICE
JUICE OF 1 ORANGE	ORANGE LIQUEUR (OPTIONAL)
ICING SUGAR, TO TASTE	

Liquidize or blend the fruit with the orange juice and 1-2 tablespoons of icing sugar. Taste for sweetness, adding lemon or more sugar, if needed.

Sieve the sauce. Add liqueur to taste, if using.

Peaches or apricots can be used instead, but you will need to remove their skins first.

THE SUMMER PUDDING CLUB

Butterscotch

Really wicked with the Toffee Ice-cream, see page 70!

Makes 1/2 pint

50G (2 OZ) BUTTER	1 TBSP GOLDEN SYRUP
150G (5 OZ) DEMERARA SUGAR	150ML (¼ PINT) EVAPORATED MILK

Melt the butter, then add the sugar and syrup and stir until they have dissolved. Pour in the evaporated milk, turn up the heat and beat until the sauce boils.

Orange

Good with Orange Ice-cream or Honey and Whisky Ice-cream, see page 70.

Makes 1/2 pint

1 TSP ARROWROOT	JUICE OF ½ LEMON
125ML (4 FL OZ) FRESH ORANGE JUICE	30ML (1 FL OZ) ORANGE LIQUEUR
	CASTER SUGAR (OPTIONAL)

Heat all the ingredients, stirring, until the sauce boils. Add a little caster sugar, if needed.

Raspberry Yoghurt Ice-cream

The yoghurt gives this ice-cream a distinct, tangy flavour. The recipe can be adapted for other soft fruit; you could also add 1 or 2 tablespoons of liqueur to the fruit purée.

Serves 4-6

225G (8 OZ) RASPBERRIES, FRESH OR FROZEN	150ML (¼ PINT) SOURED CREAM
110G (4 OZ) CASTER SUGAR	2 EGGS, SEPARATED
1–2 TSP FRESH MINT, CHOPPED	2 TBSP ICING SUGAR
150ML (¼ PINT) NATURAL YOGHURT	

Purée or blend the fruit, caster sugar and mint. Add the yoghurt, cream and egg yolks. Beat well, then pour the mixture into a plastic container and freeze, uncovered, for about 2 hours, or until it is starting to freeze around the edges.

Whisk the egg whites until stiff, add the icing sugar and whisk until the mixture forms stiff peaks.

Stir the ice-cream to break up the ice crystals and fold in the egg-white mixture. Return to the freezer. Stir two or three times during the next 3 or 4 hours. Serve straight from the freezer.

Lemon Sorbet

The addition of chopped fresh mint or lemon balm gives an interesting flavour.

Serves 4-6

2 TSP GELATINE	2 EGG WHITES
150G (5 OZ) CASTER SUGAR	1 TBSP MINT OR LEMON BALM,
½ TSP LEMON RIND	CHOPPED (OPTIONAL)
225ML (8 FL OZ) FRESH LEMON	
JUICE	

The freezer should be at its coldest setting.

Place 2 tablespoons of water in a small heatproof bowl. Sprinkle on the gelatine and place the bowl in a pan of simmering water. Leave until the liquid is clear and the gelatine has dissolved.

Put the sugar in a heavy-based pan with 200ml (7 fl oz) of water. Dissolve the sugar over a gentle heat without stirring. Bring to a boil and boil gently for 10 minutes, then stir in the dissolved gelatine, lemon rind and juice. Cover and cool.

Pour the syrup mixture into a plastic container. Cover and freeze for 1½-2 hours.

Whisk the egg whites until stiff. Remove the sorbet from the freezer and beat until smooth. Fold in the egg whites and mint or lemon balm (if using). Cover and freeze again. Serve straight from the freezer.

Apple Sorbet

Serves 4-6

4 COX'S APPLES	1 EGG WHITE
160G (5½ OZ) CASTER SUGAR	2 TBSP CALVADOS OR BRANDY
JUICE OF 1 LEMON	

Peel, core and quarter the apples, place them in a saucepan with the sugar and enough water to cover them, then poach for 20 minutes. Remove the apples from the pan, turn up the heat and reduce the liquid by boiling rapidly until it becomes thick and syrupy. Purée the apples, syrup and lemon juice in a liquidizer or food processor and add the Calvados or brandy. Allow to cool, then freeze.

When nearly frozen, after approximately 2 hours, return the sorbet to the food processor and whizz briefly. Gradually add the unwhisked egg white to the sorbet mixture with the processor switched on. It will fluff up. Return to the container and freeze again. Serve straight from the freezer.

Pear Sorbet

Substitute 4 ripe Conference or William pears for the apples, and add the juice of an extra lemon.

Strawberry Sorbet

Serves 4-6

175G (6 OZ) CASTER SUGAR	350G (12 OZ) STRAWBERRIES
JUICE OF ½ LEMON	2 EGG WHITES

Place the sugar and 570ml (1 pint) water in a pan, dissolve the sugar over a low heat and, when the liquid is clear, boil gently for 5 minutes. Add the lemon juice and leave to cool.

Liquidize or mash the strawberries to a pulp and add the syrup. Stir the mixture well. Put in a plastic container and freeze for 30 minutes, or until the syrup is beginning to solidify.

Whisk the egg whites until stiff and fold them into the half-frozen mixture. Return to the freezer.

Mango Sorbet

Prepare the sorbet as above, replacing the strawberries with 2 ripe mangoes and adding the white of only 1 egg.

CHAPTER SEVEN

*Special
Additions*

A N ALTERNATIVE title for this section could have been 'Extras
for Textures', recipes for accompaniments such as wafers and
biscuits which, in providing a contrast and balance to the acidity of
fruit or to the softness of ices and mousses, add significantly to the
whole experience.

Ratafias

Tiny, almond-based biscuits, which can be served with ice-creams, fruit desserts or as petit fours. Also good in trifles instead of sponge cake.

Makes about 40

2 EGG WHITES	110G (4 OZ) GROUND ALMONDS
150G (5 OZ) CASTER SUGAR	2 TSP GROUND RICE

Preheat the oven to 170°C/325°F/Gas 3.

Lightly oil a baking tray and cover it with rice paper or parchment paper.

In a bowl, whisk the egg whites until frothy but not stiff. Stir in the sugar, ground almonds and ground rice. Beat together with a wooden spoon until the mixture has thickened.

Using a small teaspoon, place tiny heaps on the baking tray, allowing a little room for spreading. Bake in the oven for 10-12 minutes, or until golden. Cool on a wire cooling rack.

Ginger Crisps

The flavour of ginger marries well with a lot of the summer fruits, as well as with creamy types of dessert.

Makes about 12

225G (8 OZ) PLAIN FLOUR	2 TBSP GOLDEN SYRUP
I TSP GROUND GINGER	2 TBSP BLACK TREACLE
½ TSP MIXED SPICE	I EGG, BEATEN
50G (2 OZ) BUTTER	
50G (2 OZ) SOFT DARK BROWN SUGAR	

Preheat the oven to 190°C/375°F/Gas 5.

Sift the flour, ginger and mixed spice into a bowl. In a small pan, melt the butter, sugar, syrup and treacle. Make a well in the centre of the flour and add the butter mixture. Mix well and then beat in the egg. Cover the mixture and allow to rest in the fridge, covered, for 30 minutes.

Knead the dough lightly and roll out as thinly as possible on a well-floured worktop. Cut out rounds, about 7.5cm (3 in) in diameter. Place them on lightly oiled baking trays and bake in the oven for about 12 minutes. Leave on the trays for a minute and then remove to a wire cooling rack.

Popcorn Biscuits

These elegant crisp biscuits taste very similar to popcorn.

Makes about 12

60G (2½ OZ) UNSALTED BUTTER	I TSP PLAIN FLOUR
60G (2½ OZ) PORRIDGE OATS	I TSP BAKING POWDER
IIOG (4 OZ) CASTER SUGAR	I EGG

Preheat the oven to 180°C/350°F/Gas 4. Line baking trays with parchment paper.

Melt the butter in a pan, but don't allow it to boil. Remove from the heat and stir in the oats, sugar, flour and baking powder. Beat in the egg.

Place dessertspoonsful of the mixture on the baking trays, allowing plenty of room for the mixture to spread. Only bake four biscuits at a time, keeping the rest of the mixture warm while the first batch of biscuits is cooking. Bake in the oven for 10 minutes, or until golden. Allow the biscuits to cool on the tray for 30 seconds or so and then lift them off with a fish slice or spatula and lay over a lightly oiled rolling pin to shape them. Remove, after 3 or 4 minutes, to a wire cooling rack.

If you find that the biscuits have become too cold and hard when you want to remove them from the baking trays, just put them back in the oven for a few seconds. Repeat the process until all the mixture has been used up.

Orange Thins

A very useful mixture to make, as the 'dough' can be kept in the fridge or freezer, and you can simply slice off a piece for the number of biscuits you want to make.

Makes about 25

225G (8 OZ) BUTTER, SOFTENED	PINCH OF SALT
225G (8 OZ) CASTER SUGAR	1 TSP BAKING POWDER
1 EGG, BEATEN	½ TSP VANILLA ESSENCE
1 TBSP DOUBLE CREAM	GRATED RIND OF 1 ORANGE
275G (10 OZ) PLAIN FLOUR	

Cream together the butter and sugar. Add the remaining ingredients and beat well. You can make the whole mixture in a food processor, if you have one.

Place the mixture on a sheet of parchment or greaseproof paper or clingfilm. Form the dough into a long roll or two rolls. Refrigerate the dough overnight or, if in a rush, put it in the freezer for an hour or two.

Preheat the oven to 190°C/375°F/Gas 5. Line baking trays with parchment or greaseproof paper.

When you are ready to use the dough, cut off slices as thinly as possible until you have the number of biscuits you require. Place the dough slices on the baking trays, allowing a little room for spreading. Bake in the oven for 5 minutes – the biscuits should be fairly pale in colour. Remove to a wire cooling rack.

Apricot Florentines

A lovely mixture of caramel, nuts and apricots, these biscuits will keep for up to two weeks in an airtight tin.

Makes about 16

50G (2 OZ) MIXED PEEL	50G (2 OZ) CASTER SUGAR
50G (2 OZ) FLAKED ALMONDS, LIGHTLY CRUSHED	1 TBSP PLAIN FLOUR
	1 TBSP DOUBLE CREAM
75G (3 OZ) NO-SOAK APRICOTS, CHOPPED	1 TSP LEMON JUICE
	175G (6 OZ) PLAIN OR WHITE
40G (1½ OZ) UNSALTED BUTTER	CHOCOLATE

Preheat the oven to 180°C/350°F/Gas 4. Line baking trays with parchment paper.

Mix the peel, lightly crushed almonds and chopped apricots in a bowl. In a pan, heat the butter and sugar over a low heat until the butter has melted. Remove from the heat and beat in the flour, cream and lemon juice. Place teaspoonsful of the mixture on the baking trays, leaving plenty of room for spreading, and bake in the oven for 10-15 minutes, until golden.

Leave the biscuits on the trays until cold, then remove to a wire cooling rack, turning them upside down.

Break the chocolate into pieces and melt in a bowl over a pan of simmering water. Spread the melted chocolate on the smooth side of the biscuits. When nearly set, drag a fork over the chocolate in a zig-zag fashion. Leave to set.

Presentation and Garnishing

Many flowers make pretty garnishes, and are also edible. Varieties that can be used include: geraniums, carnations, cowslips, dahlias, elderflowers, freesias, nasturtiums, primroses, roses and violets. The inclusion of fresh flowers in the presentation of a dessert can transform something fairly ordinary into a spectacular-looking dish.

Chocolate cups can be used as edible containers for mousses, ice-creams and sorbets. Pour melted chocolate, plain or white, into fluted paper cases and coat the base and sides. Pour off any excess chocolate. Leave to set, then apply a second coat to the base. When set, peel away the paper case.

Whole almonds, brazils or walnut halves, strawberries, orange segments, grapes or cherries can be dipped, with the aid of forks, into melted chocolate and left on greaseproof paper to set.

If using bay or rose leaves as a mould, first wash and dry the leaves, then brush the back of the leaves with melted chocolate. Allow to set and apply a second coat. When completely set, carefully peel the original leaf away to leave the chocolate one.

Whole fruits, e.g. strawberries, raspberries, grapes and cherries, or segments of fruit can be used as decorative garnishes. Mint leaves, rosebuds, violets or primroses can be rinsed and dried, then brushed with lightly beaten egg white and dusted with caster sugar. Lay them on greaseproof paper and leave at room temperature to dry out for an hour or so.

Caramelized Fruits and Nuts

SELECTION OF CHERRIES, GRAPES,	ALMONDS, HAZELNUTS — ABOUT
STRAWBERRIES, SEGMENTS OF	30 ITEMS IN ALL
SATSUMA, BRAZILNUTS, WHOLE	200G (7 OZ) GRANULATED SUGAR

If using grapes or cherries, keep them in small clusters; if using strawberries, keep the stems on. Put the sugar in a pan, add 175ml (6 fl oz) of water and heat gently, so that the sugar dissolves slowly; give the pan an occasional shake. When the sugar has dissolved, turn up the heat and boil until the liquid becomes a pale gold syrup.

Remove the pan from the heat and dip it into a bowl of cold water, to prevent any further cooking. Spear the fruit or nuts on a fork, one at a time, and dip into the caramel, allowing any excess caramel to drip back into the pan. With the help of another fork, ease the fruit or nut off on to a baking tray lined with greaseproof paper. Leave to set.

Biscuit Baskets

These make good containers for fresh fruit, ice-creams or sorbets.

Makes 8 baskets

75G (3 OZ) BUTTER	3 EGG WHITES
75G (3 OZ) CASTER SUGAR	75G (3 OZ) PLAIN FLOUR, SIFTED

Preheat the oven to 220°C/425°F/Gas 7. Lightly oil and line a baking tray with parchment paper.

In a pan, melt the butter, add the sugar and stir over a gentle heat until the sugar has dissolved. Gradually beat in the egg whites, using a balloon whisk, and fold in the sifted flour. Bake two biscuits at a time, for 4-5 minutes. The biscuits should be just brown around the edges. While still warm, curl the biscuit rounds over lightly oiled, upturned jam-jars. Leave until cold. If the bisuits are not crisp at this stage, put them back in the oven, still on the jam-jars, for another minute or two.

Brandy Snap Baskets

Another suitable container for ice-creams, mousses, fruit or sorbets. But don't fill them until just before they are required.

Makes 8 baskets

50G (2 OZ) BUTTER	½ TSP GROUND GINGER
2 TBSP GOLDEN SYRUP	GRATED RIND OF ½ LEMON
50G (2 OZ) CASTER SUGAR	I TSP BRANDY
50G (2 OZ) PLAIN FLOUR, SIFTED	

Preheat the oven to 180°C/350°F/Gas 4. Line baking trays with parchment paper.

In a pan, melt the butter, syrup and sugar over a low heat, stir until smooth, then remove from the heat. Add the sifted flour and ginger, and stir in the lemon rind and brandy. Leave to cool for 2-3 minutes.

Put teaspoonsful of the mixture on to the baking trays, allowing plenty of room for spreading. Cook three or four biscuits at a time. Bake in the oven for 7-10 minutes.

Remove from the oven when the biscuits are a golden-brown colour. Leave to cool for about 30 seconds, then lift them off the baking trays with a palette knife or fish slice and shape them over an upturned, lightly oiled jam-jar.

When the biscuits are cool, remove them to a wire cooling rack. Once they are completely cold, store in an airtight tin.

Coconut Wafers

For those who are lovers of coconut, these wafers go well with fresh fruit or fruit-based desserts.

Makes about 10

50G (2 OZ) BUTTER	2 TSP LEMON JUICE
50G (2 OZ) CASTER SUGAR	50G (2 OZ) PLAIN FLOUR, SIFTED
I TBSP GOLDEN SYRUP	25G (I OZ) DESICCATED COCONUT

Preheat the oven to 180°C/350°F/Gas 4. Lightly oil baking trays.

Cream the butter and sugar until pale and fluffy, then beat in the syrup. Add the lemon juice, sifted flour and coconut. Drop teaspoonsful of mixture on to the baking trays, allowing plenty of room for spreading. Bake in the oven for about 10 minutes, or until the edges of the wafers are golden but the centres are still pale. Cool slightly, then remove to a wire cooling rack until completely cold.

CHAPTER EIGHT

Light and Luscious

W<small>E ARE NOW</small> getting to some seriously delicious desserts. Puddings in this category have attracted comments such as 'naughty', 'wicked' and 'outrageous'! They are deceptive, because they are so light and delicious that no one can imagine that they contain much in the way of calories or sugar. But be not deterred, dear reader. Remember the Pudding Club's ethic – it is not what you eat that does you harm or good; it is your attitude of mind while ingesting the stuff. With a joyful and zestful heart, the experience is entirely benign!

Raspberry Atholl Brose

A Scottish dessert, which is equally good made with chopped strawberries. You could use brandy or an orange-based liqueur instead of the whisky.

Serves 4-6

275ML (½ PINT) DOUBLE CREAM	3 TBSP RUNNY HONEY, PLUS EXTRA
50G (2 OZ) PINHEAD (FINE) OAT-	TO DECORATE
MEAL, TOASTED, PLUS EXTRA TO	75ML (3 FL OZ) WHISKY
DECORATE	225G (8 OZ) RASPBERRIES

Whip the cream until firm. Stir in the cold toasted oatmeal and honey. Chill.

Shortly before serving, stir in the whisky. You can then stir in the raspberries, but it does look prettier if you layer the cream mixture and the raspberries in a glass bowl or individual glasses. Decorate the top with an extra drizzle of honey and toasted oatmeal.

White Chocolate Mousse

Try to buy good quality white chocolate. Serve with a plain chocolate sauce or an orange sauce. You could also serve it with a bowl of slightly sweetened soft fruits.

Serves 4-6

1 TBSP MILK	LEVEL DSTSP CASTER SUGAR
110G (4 OZ) WHITE CHOCOLATE	A FEW DROPS OF VANILLA ESSENCE
2 EGGS, SEPARATED, PLUS AN EXTRA	5G (¼ OZ) GELATINE
EGG WHITE	125ML (4 FL OZ) DOUBLE CREAM

In a pan, stir the milk and chocolate, roughly broken, over a gentle heat until the chocolate has melted.

Beat the egg yolks and sugar in a bowl until pale and creamy, then add the vanilla essence.

Put 2 tablespoons of water in a cup and sprinkle on the gelatine. Allow to soak for a few minutes.

Stir the warm chocolate mixture into the eggs and sugar. Put the cup with the gelatine into a pan of simmering water, and when the liquid is clear, add it to the chocolate mixture.

Refrigerate the chocolate mixture for 30 minutes, until just starting to set. Meanwhile, in separate bowls, whisk the egg whites and whip the cream. Remove the chocolate mixture from the fridge, and fold in the cream and egg whites. Pour into individual glasses or a nice glass bowl.

Mocha and Walnut Chiffon Pie

Plain chocolate biscuits and chopped walnuts make the base for this light coffee-flavoured dessert.

Serves 4-6

Base

110G (4 OZ) PLAIN CHOCOLATE DIGESTIVES	PLUS EXTRA TO DECORATE
25G (1 OZ) WALNUTS, CHOPPED,	50G (2 OZ) BUTTER, MELTED

Filling

110G (4 OZ) CASTER OR SOFT BROWN SUGAR	PINCH OF SALT
2 TSP GELATINE	2 TSP TIA MARIA, OR ORANGE OR LEMON JUICE
1 TBSP COFFEE GRANULES	WHIPPED CREAM AND GRATED
2 EGGS, SEPARATED	CHOCOLATE, TO DECORATE

To make the biscuit base, crush the biscuits finely and stir in the walnuts and butter. Use to line the base and sides of an 18cm (7 in) pie plate or loose-bottomed flan tin.

For the filling, mix 50g (2 oz) of the sugar with the gelatine in a small bowl or cup. Put the coffee into a measuring jug, add 3 tablespoons of boiling water and stir until the coffee has dissolved. Bring the liquid level up to 225ml (8 fl oz) with water.

Pour the coffee into a bowl and stand over a pan of simmering water. Beat in the egg yolks and stir in the gelatine mixture. Add a pinch of salt. Cook over a gentle heat, stirring until the mixture thickens slightly. Don't allow it to boil. Remove from the heat, cool a little, then refrigerate for 20–30 minutes, or until the mixture is just starting to set. Stir in the Tia Maria or fruit juice.

Whisk the egg whites and gradually add the remaining sugar, continuing to whisk until thick and glossy. Fold in the custard mixture and combine well. Pour the mixture into the biscuit shell and chill for 1-2 hours. Decorate with whipped cream and extra walnuts and grated chocolate, if liked.

Chocolate and Bay Creams

This unusual marrying of chocolate and bay leaves works extremely well. The mixture is quite rich, so a little goes a long way.

Serves 4-6

110G (4 OZ) GRANULATED SUGAR	75G (3 OZ) GOOD QUALITY PLAIN
125ML (4 FL OZ) DRY WHITE WINE	CHOCOLATE
1 TBSP LEMON JUICE	4 FRESH OR 2 DRIED BAY LEAVES
275ML (½ PINT) DOUBLE CREAM	

Mix the sugar, wine and lemon juice in a pan and heat gently until the sugar has dissolved. Add the cream, chocolate, roughly broken, and bay leaves and bring to a boil, stirring. Continue to stir until the chocolate has melted, then simmer for 15 minutes.

Allow to cool a little, remove the bay leaves and pour the mixture into ramekins or other suitably small dishes. Cover and refrigerate.

Blackcurrant and Mint Soufflé

You can, of course, substitute strawberries, raspberries or blackberries for the blackcurrants, but I would only use the mint with blackcurrants. Try using evaporated milk as an alternative to the cream.

Serves 6-8

1 TBSP GELATINE	1 TBSP LEMON JUICE
350G (12 OZ) BLACKCURRANTS	3 EGGS, SEPARATED
110G (4 OZ) CASTER SUGAR	125ML (4 FL OZ) DOUBLE CREAM
8 MINT LEAVES, PLUS EXTRA TO	OR EVAPORATED MILK, PLUS
DECORATE	EXTRA TO DECORATE

Place 3 tablespoons of water in a cup and sprinkle on the gelatine. Stand in a pan of simmering water and leave until the gelatine has dissolved and is clear. Cool slightly.

In a large pan, gently stew the blackcurrants, sugar, mint and lemon juice with 1-2 tablespoons of water until the fruit is soft. Allow to cool a little, then put in a food processor or liquidizer and blend until smooth. Sieve out the seeds. Measure out 150ml (¼ pint) of fruit purée.

Whisk the egg yolks until thick and creamy, add 1 tablespoon of this mixture to the gelatine and stir well, then whisk into the remaining egg-yolk mixture. Stir in the measured blackcurrant purée. Put in the fridge for 10-20 minutes, until just starting to set.

Whip the cream until it just holds its shape, then fold it into the blackcurrant mixture and blend evenly. Whisk the egg whites until stiff but not dry, and with a metal spoon carefully fold into the blackcurrant and cream. Spoon the mixture into a soufflé dish

Raspberry Atholl Brose is a Scottish dessert which makes good use of Scotland's traditional spirit.
See page 92.

When summer weather is disappointing, this Plum and
Cinnamon Cobbler is warm and spiced.
See page 105.

The addition of lime juice to the filling of Lemon and
Lime Meringue Pie gives it an extra piquancy.
See page 106.

 The cherries in these Chocolate and Cherry Puffs are given
extra flavour by soaking them in brandy or Kirsch.
See page 115.

or glass bowls. Allow to set in the fridge, covered, for 2-3 hours. Decorate with swirls of whipped cream and mint leaves.

Orange Mousse

A light and low-fat dessert, with yoghurt taking the place of cream.

Serves 4-6

10G (½ OZ) GELATINE	275ML (½ PINT) THICK NATURAL
250ML (9 FL OZ) FRESH ORANGE	GREEK YOGHURT
JUICE	2 EGG WHITES, WHISKED
GRATED RIND OF 1 ORANGE	RUNNY HONEY, TO TASTE
1 TBSP ORANGE LIQUEUR	(OPTIONAL)
(OPTIONAL)	

Put 2 tablespoons of water in a cup and sprinkle on the gelatine. Allow to soak for a few minutes, then place the cup in a pan of simmering water, until the gelatine has dissolved. Add to the orange juice, rind and liqueur, if using. Gently beat in the yoghurt. Refrigerate for 30 minutes, or until just beginning to set.

Remove the mixture from the fridge and fold in the egg whites. Add a little honey, if desired. Pour into a glass bowl or individual glasses and allow to set for 2-3 hours. Serve with orange segments, half dipped in melted chocolate, and home-made biscuits.

Cherry Crème Brûlée

A layer of cherries is to be found beneath the rich egg custard, once you have cracked open the caramel topping.

Serves 4-6

350G (12 OZ) CHERRIES, STONED WEIGHT	5 EGG YOLKS
	I TSP VANILLA ESSENCE
110G (4 OZ) CASTER SUGAR	570ML (I PINT) DOUBLE CREAM
2 TSP ARROWROOT	3-4 TBSP DEMERARA SUGAR
2 TBSP KIRSCH (OPTIONAL)	

Place the cherries in a pan with 150ml (¼ pint) of water and 50g (2 oz) of the caster sugar, and cook over a gentle heat until the sugar has dissolved, stirring occasionally. Turn up the heat and allow to bubble gently for 2-3 minutes. Mix the arrowroot with 2 teaspoons of cold water and stir it into the warm cherries. Leave to cool, then add the Kirsch, if using. Spoon the cherries into ramekins or a shallow ovenproof dish, cover and refrigerate for 2-3 hours.

Mix the egg yolks thoroughly with the remaining caster sugar and the vanilla essence. Heat the cream to boiling point and slowly whisk into the egg-yolk mixture. Strain through a sieve into a clean pan, then cook over a gentle heat, stirring all the time with a wooden spoon, for about 10 minutes, or until the mixture coats the back of the spoon. Do not allow it to boil. Cover and leave the mixture to cool. When it has cooled and thickened, pour it over the cherries. Sprinkle the demerara sugar thickly over the cherry and cream mixture.

Preheat a grill until it is really hot, place the ramekins under the grill and cook until the sugar topping has melted and looks shiny. Cool and then chill until needed.

Cream Cheese and Almond Loaf

A luxurious mixture of cream cheese, honey and almond, baked together and served in slices when cool. This recipe can be made 1 or 2 days before it is needed.

Serves 6-8

25G (1 OZ) UNSALTED BUTTER	3 EGGS, SEPARATED
75G (3 OZ) CASTER SUGAR	55ML (2 FL OZ) SINGLE CREAM
1 TBSP RUNNY HONEY	25G (1 OZ) PLAIN FLOUR
225G (8 OZ) CREAM CHEESE	50G (2 OZ) FLAKED ALMONDS,
1 TSP VANILLA ESSENCE	CHOPPED

Preheat the oven to 170°C/325°F/Gas 3.

Lightly butter a 450g (1 lb) loaf or cake tin. Put the butter, half the sugar, honey, cream cheese, vanilla essence and egg yolks in a food processor and whizz until well blended. Add the cream and flour and whizz again.

In a bowl, beat the egg whites until stiff but not dry, and gradually whisk in the remaining sugar. With a metal spoon, stir the egg white mixture into the cream cheese mixture, doing this in two or three batches. Finally, stir in the chopped almonds.

Pour the mixture into the tin and bake in the oven for 45-60 minutes, or until just set. Turn the oven off and leave the cheese loaf to cool in the oven.

Serve at room temperature, lightly dusted with icing sugar and with a jug of fruit sauce (see pages 73-75) as an accompaniment.

Berry Cheese Mousse

To present this pudding at its best, use an 870ml (1½ pint) ring mould; alternatively, line a similar-sized soufflé dish with clingfilm. Any mixture of fresh soft fruits will do, or you could use a bag of defrosted summer fruits, available from most supermarkets.

Serves 4-6

110G (4 OZ) CASTER SUGAR	GRATED RIND AND JUICE OF ½
110G (4 OZ) BLACKCURRANTS,	LEMON
STALKS REMOVED	GRATED RIND AND JUICE OF ½
110G (4 OZ) RASPBERRIES, HULLED	ORANGE
110G (4 OZ) REDCURRANTS, STALKS	225G (8 OZ) COTTAGE CHEESE
REMOVED	175ML (6 FL OZ) DOUBLE CREAM
5 TEASPOONS GELATINE	1 LARGE EGG, SEPARATED

Dissolve 50g (2 oz) of the sugar in 150ml (¼ pint) of water, add the prepared fruit and cook slowly until the fruit is soft but not mushy. Remove from the heat. Put 2 tablespoons of water in a cup and sprinkle on 2 teaspoons of gelatine. Allow to stand for 5 minutes and then place the cup in a pan of simmering water. Leave until the gelatine has dissolved and is clear. Stir it into the fruit mixture. Allow to cool, then pour into the mould. Chill for about 1 hour, or until set.

In a food processor or blender, combine the orange and lemon rind and juice, the remaining sugar, cottage cheese, cream and egg yolk. (You could also do this by hand, but you would need to sieve the cottage cheese first.) Prepare the remaining 3 teaspoons of gelatine as described above, then add to the cream mixture and whizz up again.

Turn the mixture into a bowl. Whisk the egg white until stiff, then fold it into the cream mixture. Pour into a ring mould and chill until set, about 1 hour. Unmould the mousse on to a serving plate; you may need to dip the base of the mould into hot water for a second or two first.

Cranberry Velvet

Any other soft fruit could be used instead of the cranberries. Garnish with a few whole fruit that have been dipped in lightly beaten egg white, rolled in caster sugar and left to harden on greaseproof paper.

Serves 4-6

225G (8 OZ) CRANBERRIES, PLUS A FEW TO DECORATE	2 TBSP LEMON JUICE (OPTIONAL)
	3 LEVEL TSP GELATINE
75G (3 OZ) CASTER SUGAR, PLUS 2 TBSP EXTRA	4 TBSP DOUBLE CREAM, PLUS EXTRA TO DECORATE
3 EGG YOLKS	FROSTED FRUIT AND MINT LEAVES,
425ML (1 PINT) MILK	TO DECORATE

In a pan, bring the cranberries to a boil with 6 tablespoons of water. Simmer until the fruit 'pops'. Remove from the heat and add 75g (3oz) of sugar, stirring until it dissolves. Allow to cool. Beat together the egg yolks and the extra 2 tablespoons of caster sugar. Heat the milk and gradually pour on to the egg yolks, stirring constantly. Return this mixture to the pan and cook, stirring all the time, until the sauce coats the back of a wooden spoon. Don't allow it to boil. Remove from the heat and cool.

In a food processor or blender, purée the fruit and custard mixture, then push through a sieve.

Put the lemon juice or 2 tablespoons of water in a cup or small bowl and sprinkle on the gelatine. Allow to stand for 5 minutes and then place the cup in a pan of simmering water. Leave until the gelatine has dissolved and is clear. Leave to cool for 5–10 minutes, then stir into the cold purée.

Whip the cream until it forms soft peaks and fold gently into the cranberry mixture. Pour into attractive glasses or a glass bowl. Cover and refrigerate. Decorate with swirls of cream, frosted fruit and mint leaves.

CHAPTER NINE

Warm and Wonderful

Tʜɪs sᴇᴄᴛɪᴏɴ is a concession to those cynics who have been sniggering at the vision presented so far in this book – of the British summer as a never-ending succession of long warm days in which to enjoy all these luxurious concoctions. To allow for the possibility that there might occasionally be a less than sunny day, we have selected ten recipes that will provide a generous dollop of compensation for those coming in out of the cold.

Raspberry Custard Tart

This is an old-fashioned custard tart, with the addition of a few raspberries scattered over the pastry base.

Serves 4-6

Pastry

175G (6 OZ) PLAIN FLOUR	75G (3 OZ) BUTTER (OR ½ BUTTER,
¼ TSP SALT	½ LARD), DICED

Filling

225ML (8 FL OZ) CREAMY MILK	2 TBSP RUNNY HONEY
2 EGGS	175G (6 OZ) FRESH RASPBERRIES
1 EGG YOLK	GROUND NUTMEG OR MACE
75G (3 OZ) CASTER SUGAR, OR	

Preheat the oven to 190°C/375°F/Gas 5.

To make the pastry, sift the flour and salt together and rub in the diced butter until the mixture resembles fine breadcrumbs. Add enough water to make a stiff dough. Roll out and line a greased 20cm (8 in) cake tin or earthenware dish. Put in the fridge to rest for 30 minutes.

In a small pan, bring the milk to a simmer. Put the eggs and egg yolk in a mixing bowl, add the sugar or honey and beat well. Slowly stir in the hot milk.

Scatter the raspberries over the pastry base and strain the egg custard over them. Sprinkle the nutmeg or mace over the top.

Bake in the oven for 10 minutes, then lower the heat to 150°C/300°F/Gas 2 and cook for a further 15-20 minutes, or until just set. You can serve this tart warm, but it is also delicious cold.

Plum and Cinnamon Cobbler

A very quick and comforting pudding to eat on a not-so-warm summer's day.

Serves 6-8

700G (1½ LB) PLUMS, STONED WEIGHT	175G (6 OZ) PLAIN FLOUR
JUICE AND RIND OF 1 ORANGE	2 TSP BAKING POWDER
75G (3 OZ) SOFT LIGHT BROWN SUGAR	PINCH OF SALT
	1 TSP GROUND CINNAMON
1 CINNAMON STICK (OPTIONAL)	125ML (4 FL OZ) MILK
75G (3 OZ) BUTTER	1 TBSP DEMERARA SUGAR

Preheat the oven to 220°C /425°F/Gas 7.

Halve the plums and discard the stones. Put the plums, orange juice, brown sugar and cinnamon stick, if using, in a large pan and slowly bring to a boil. Simmer for 3-4 minutes, covered, then allow to cool in the pan for 45-60 minutes. Pour the fruit into a casserole dish, approx. 23 x 6cm (9 x 2½ in) deep.

For the cobbler topping, rub the butter into the flour, baking powder and salt, until it resembles fine breadcrumbs; alternatively, whizz it up in a food processor. Add the ground cinnamon and orange rind and stir in the milk until you have a sticky, dough-like mixture. Spoon the mixture in dollops over the fruit and sprinkle generously with demerara sugar. Bake in the oven for 25-30 minutes, or until golden. The cobbler is best served warm, with thick cream.

Variations

Rhubarb, blackcurrant or blackberry and apple could be used instead of the plums (no need to precook the fruit). If using gooseberry or apricot, lightly cook the fruit first.

Lemon and Lime Meringue Pie

The addition of fresh lime juice to the filling of this well-known pie makes it even more delicious. You will need a prebaked 20cm (8 in) shortcrust pastry shell.

Serves 4-6

225G (8OZ) READY-MADE SHORT-CRUST PASTRY	JUICE AND GRATED RIND OF 1 LIME
	25G (1 OZ) BUTTER
25G (1 OZ) CORNFLOUR	2 EGGS, SEPARATED
25G (1 OZ) CASTER SUGAR	EXTRA 110G (4 OZ) CASTER SUGAR
JUICE OF 1 SMALL LEMON	

Bake the shortcrust pastry shell in advance.

Preheat the oven to 170°C/325°F/Gas 3.

To make the filling, mix the cornflour with 1 tablespoon of water (taken from 275ml/½ pint) until you have a smooth paste. Heat the remaining water, 25g (1 oz) of caster sugar, lemon juice, lime juice and rind and bring to a boil. Gradually beat the lemon sauce into the cornflour mixture and return to the pan. Bring back to the boil, stirring continuously, and allow to simmer for 3-4 minutes. Remove the pan from the heat and add the butter, stirring until it has melted. Allow to cool slightly, then beat in the egg yolks. Taste for sweetness, but don't forget it should be fairly tart to balance the sweetness of the meringue topping. Pour the mixture into the prepared pastry case and bake in the oven for 10 minutes.

Meanwhile, beat the egg whites until very stiff and beat in the 110g (4 oz) of caster sugar, a tablespoon at a time. Cover the lemon filling completely with meringue, piling it into soft peaks. For a soft meringue, return the pie to the oven for 10 minutes. For a crisper finish, reduce the oven temperature to 140°C/275°F/Gas 1 and bake for 30-40 minutes. Serve warm.

Creamy Blackcurrant Pie

A deep fruit pie, where the fruit is enriched with a cream and egg mixture added towards the end of the cooking time. If you find blackcurrants hard to come by, use raspberries or a bag of ready-prepared summer fruits, available from most supermarkets.

Serves 4-6

350G (12 OZ) READY-MADE PUFF PASTRY, OR A SWEET SHORT-CRUST IF YOU PREFER	175G (6 OZ) SOFT BROWN SUGAR, PLUS A LITTLE CASTER SUGAR
A LITTLE EGG WHITE, BEATEN	1 TSP CHOPPED MINT (OPTIONAL)
450G (1 LB) BLACKCURRANTS	225ML (8 FL OZ) WHIPPING CREAM
	2 LARGE EGG YOLKS

Preheat the oven to 220°C/425°F/Gas 7.

Roll out a little more than half of the pastry and line a greased 3-5cm (1½-2 in) deep pie dish. Brush the pastry with a little beaten egg white, to prevent it becoming soggy. Pile in the blackcurrants, soft brown sugar and mint (if using). Make a pie lid with the remaining pastry, leaving a small hole in the centre. Decorate with pastry leaves made from the pastry trimmings. Brush on some egg white and sprinkle caster sugar over the top. Bake in the oven for 15 minutes, then lower the heat to 190°C/375°F/Gas 5 for a further 25-30 minutes.

When the pie has been cooking for 30 minutes, heat the cream in a pan to boiling point and beat it into the egg yolks. Remove the pie from the oven and pour the cream mixture into the central hole through a funnel. Do this slowly and stop before the pie overflows. Return to the oven for a further 5 minutes. Serve warm.

Plums in Overcoats

An adaptation of apple dumplings. If you don't like marzipan, just fill the plums with demerara sugar and a little cinnamon.

Serves 4

225G (8 OZ) PLAIN FLOUR	8 LARGE RIPE VICTORIA PLUMS
PINCH OF SALT	110G (4 OZ) GOOD QUALITY
110G (4 OZ) MARGARINE (OR ½	MARZIPAN
BUTTER, ½ LARD)	CASTER SUGAR, TO DECORATE

Preheat the oven to 200°C/400°F/Gas 6.

Sift the flour with a pinch of salt into a bowl and rub in the margarine until the mixture resembles fine breadcrumbs. Add enough cold water to make a stiff dough. Cover and allow to rest in the fridge for 30 minutes. Divide the pastry into eight portions, keeping back a little for decoration.

Wash and dry the plums, then cut them in half and remove the stones. Divide the marzipan into eight, roll into balls and sandwich together the plums and marzipan.

Roll each portion of pastry into rounds, place a plum in the centre of each and work the pastry around each plum to enclose it. Place the plum dumplings on a lightly oiled baking tray, seam side down and decorate the tops with pastry leaves made from the spare pastry. Brush with water and sprinkle with the caster sugar. Bake in the oven for 25-30 minutes. Serve warm with custard, or a bowl of whipped cream, and demerara sugar.

Blackberry and Cream Cheese Croissant

The cream cheese mixture works well as a pancake filling, but for a speedy and scrumptious dessert (or a breakfast treat) ready-made croissants are ideal.

Serves 1

I CROISSANT, PREFERABLY FROZEN	I TSP CASTER SUGAR OR SOFT
25G (I OZ) CREAM CHEESE	BROWN SUGAR
A LITTLE GRATED ORANGE RIND	PINCH OF CINNAMON
AND JUICE	50G (2 OZ) BLACKBERRIES

Halve the croissant lengthways (this is most easily done if the croissant is frozen). Mix together the cream cheese, orange rind and juice, sugar and cinnamon and beat well. Spread this mixture on to the frozen croissant. Allow the croissant to thaw – this will only take 15-20 minutes – then scatter on the blackberries. Sandwich the two croissant halves together and bake in a fairly hot oven for about 8 minutes.

You can substitute raspberries, strawberries, stoned cherries or blackcurrants for the blackberries.

Peach Batter Pudding

Not as heavy as it might sound, this is a delicate pudding that can be eaten warm or cold. You will need a 30-35cm (12-14 in) round earthenware dish or cake tin.

Serves 4

Base

5 LEVEL TBSP PLAIN FLOUR	½ TSP BAKING POWDER
4 HEAPED TBSP CASTER SUGAR	1 LARGE EGG
3 TBSP MILK	2 LARGE, FAIRLY RIPE PEACHES OR
2 TBSP SUNFLOWER OIL	NECTARINES, SLICED

Topping

1 LARGE EGG, BEATEN	60G (2½ OZ) BUTTER, MELTED
75G (3 OZ) CASTER SUGAR	

Preheat the oven to 180°C /350°F/Gas 4.

Beat together all the ingredients for the base except the peaches or nectarines. Lightly grease the ovenproof dish. Pour in the batter, then arrange the sliced fruit all over the base. Bake in the oven for 25 minutes.

In the meantime, prepare the topping. Mix the beaten egg and sugar into the cooled, melted butter. Remove the pudding from the oven and spread the topping over the base. Bake for a further 15 minutes.

You could use sliced apples, pears or apricots instead of the peaches.

Apricot and Almond Crumble

Coating the apricots in the sugary butter mixture first is well worth the effort. You could also use the apricots, cooked this way, as a filling for a pie.

Serves 4-6

50G (2 OZ) UNSALTED BUTTER	450G (I LB) FRESH APRICOTS,
175G (6 OZ) CASTER SUGAR	HALVED AND STONED

Topping

150G (5 OZ) BUTTER, DICED	DEMERARA SUGAR AND FLAKED
110G (4 OZ) PLAIN FLOUR	ALMONDS, TO DECORATE
110G (4 OZ) GROUND ALMONDS	(OPTIONAL)
50G (2 OZ) CASTER SUGAR OR SOFT	
BROWN SUGAR	

Preheat the oven to 180°C /300°F/Gas 4.

In a large frying pan, melt the butter and stir in the sugar. Over a low heat, allow the sugar to dissolve, giving the mixture an occasional stir. Add the apricots and coat them in the sugary mixture, but don't allow them to cook. Put the fruit into a suitable ovenproof dish.

For the crumble topping, rub the butter into the flour and ground almonds until the mixture resembles fine breadcrumbs. (You can do this in a food processor.) Add the sugar and stir until well combined. Pile the crumble over the apricots and sprinkle with a little demerara sugar and flaked almonds, if liked. Bake in the oven for 35-45 minutes, until the topping is golden.

Fresh Pineapple Fritters

If possible, steep the prepared fresh pineapple rings in 2 tablespoons of Kirsch and a sprinkling of sugar a few hours or the night before you make the fritters.

Serves 4-6

110G (4 OZ) PLAIN FLOUR	1 MEDIUM PINEAPPLE, CUT INTO
2 EGGS	RINGS AND CORE REMOVED,
PINCH OF SALT	PREPARED AS ABOVE
1 TBSP GROUNDNUT OIL	CASTER SUGAR, TO DECORATE
UP TO 275ML (½ PINT) MILK	

In a large bowl, mix the flour, 1 whole egg, 1 egg yolk (keep the white), salt and oil, then beat in about half of the milk. (This can all be done in a food processor, but be careful not to over-beat.) Continue to beat in more milk until the mixture is the consistency of thick pouring cream. Beat the egg white until it forms stiff peaks and fold into the batter.

Drain the pineapple well, but don't throw away the juices. Dip the rings into the batter, then fry in hot oil until golden brown. You will need to cook them in two or three batches. Drain on kitchen paper and sprinkle with caster sugar.

If you do have some Kirsch juices, put these in a little pan with 125ml (4 fl oz) of orange or pineapple juice and a little orange rind and 50g (2 oz) of sugar, bring to a boil and thicken with 2 teaspoons of arrowroot. Serve in a separate bowl as an accompaniment.

Raspberry Queen of Puddings

A glorious twist on an old favourite. This light pudding would be very welcome served warm on a cool summer's day.

Serves 4-6

110G (4 OZ) BREADCRUMBS OR DICED BREAD	50G (2 OZ) BUTTER
	½ TSP ALMOND ESSENCE
50G (2 OZ) GROUND ALMONDS	4 EGG YOLKS
570ML (1 PINT) MILK	50G (2 OZ) CASTER SUGAR
FINELY GRATED RIND OF 1 SMALL ORANGE	450G (1 LB) FRESH RASPBERRIES

Meringue Topping

4 EGG WHITES	225G (8 OZ) CASTER SUGAR

Preheat the oven to 180°C/350°F/Gas 4.

Mix together the breadcrumbs or bread and the ground almonds, then spread them in an even layer in a greased 1.2 litre (2 pint) pie dish. Heat the milk, orange rind, butter and almond essence in a pan, and when the butter has melted beat the mixture into the egg yolks and sugar. Pour over the breadcrumbs and allow to stand for 10 minutes. Bake in the oven for 20-25 minutes. Remove from the oven and allow to cool for 20-30 minutes. Scatter on the raspberries. Reduce the oven temperature to 150°C/300°F/Gas 2.

To make the topping, whisk the egg whites until stiff, then gradually beat in the sugar, whisking at high speed all the time. Spread the meringue on to the raspberries and return to the oven for 35-45 minutes, or until pale golden and crisp.

CHAPTER TEN

Chocolate

No book about desserts could possibly not have a recipe that used chocolate. This one has ten recipes, and we have given them a section to themselves so that the really devoted chocolate-lovers don't have to search through the index, but can go straight to their heart's desire. Notice that we eschew the word 'choco-holic', a term which is both inaccurate and misleading. It implies that to indulge your love for chocolate regularly and passionately is bad for you. Let us be clear: chocolate is wonderful, inspiring stuff, life-enhancing in every way. It is a vital part of anyone's diet, and therefore only addictive in the sense that breathing or sleeping are addictions – and much more pleasurable! Now you may read on, and no more of this 'chocoholic' nonsense, please.

Chocolate and Cherry Puffs

A combination of cherries in choux buns, smothered in a chocolate sauce. You could use chopped strawberries or raspberries instead of the cherries.

Makes 8

225G (8 OZ) RIPE CHERRIES, STONED	150ML (¼ PINT) WATER AND MILK, IN EQUAL QUANTITIES
4 TBSP BRANDY OR KIRSCH	2 EGGS, BEATEN
60G (2½ OZ) PLAIN FLOUR	225–275ML (8–10 FL OZ) DOUBLE
PINCH OF SALT	CREAM, WHIPPED, OR VANILLA
50G (2 OZ) BUTTER, DICED	ICE-CREAM

Preheat the oven to 220°C/425°F/Gas 7.

Soak the prepared cherries in brandy or Kirsch for 2–3 hours.

Sift the flour with a pinch of salt. In a pan, heat the butter with the water and milk. When the butter has melted, bring the liquid to a boil, remove from the heat and quickly add the flour, beating with a wooden spoon until the mixture forms a ball and leaves the sides of the pan. Leave to cool for about 5 minutes. Gradually beat in the eggs, a little at a time, until the dough is shiny and will fall from the spoon.

Place 8 individual tablespoonsful of the mixture on a baking tray, allowing a little room for spreading, and bake for 20 minutes. Remove from the oven, pierce each one with a sharp knife, then return to the oven for a further 5–10 minutes, until crisp and golden. Remove to a wire cooling rack.

Before serving, cut off the top third of each bun. Place some whipped cream or ice-cream in the bottom portion and some cherries and juices on top. Cover with the tops and pour over a little warm chocolate sauce (see page 74). Serve the rest separately.

Variations

Add 2 or 3 tablespoons of icing sugar or a few drops of vanilla essence to the whipped cream.

Add a little brandy, coffee or orange liqueur to the chocolate sauce.

Chocolate Mousse

A simple but impressive mousse which looks lovely served in pretty glasses. A few chopped strawberries, raspberries, peaches or cherries could be put in the bottom of the serving dishes before pouring over the mousse.

Serves 6-8

225G (8 OZ) GOOD QUALITY PLAIN CHOCOLATE	2–3 TSP COFFEE OR ORANGE LIQUEUR (OPTIONAL)
25G (1 OZ) UNSALTED BUTTER	WHIPPED CREAM, WHOLE FRUIT,
4 EGGS, SEPARATED	MINT LEAVES OR TOASTED
A FEW DROPS OF VANILLA ESSENCE	ALMONDS, TO DECORATE

Put the chocolate and butter in a bowl over a pan of simmering water. Leave to melt, stirring only occasionally. Remove the pan from the heat, once the mixture has melted, and stir in the egg yolks, vanilla essence and liqueur, if using.

Beat the egg whites until stiff but not dry. Gently fold the egg whites into the chocolate, doing this in three or four batches.

Spoon the mousse into glasses or a serving bowl. Decorate with a little whipped cream, whole fruit, mint leaves or toasted almonds.

Chocolate and Raspberry Mousse Cake

A soft cake with a fudgy, mousse-like centre.

Serves 6-8

175G (6 OZ) GOOD QUALITY PLAIN CHOCOLATE	I TSP VANILLA ESSENCE
175G (6 OZ) UNSALTED BUTTER	GRATED RIND OF I ORANGE
175G (6 OZ) CASTER SUGAR	250G (8 OZ) RASPBERRIES (FRESH OR FROZEN)
5 MEDIUM EGGS, SEPARATED	150ML (¼ PINT) DOUBLE CREAM, WHIPPED
50G (2 OZ) PLAIN FLOUR	
75G (3 OZ) GROUND HAZELNUTS OR ALMONDS	

Preheat the oven to 180°C/350°F/Gas 4.

Lightly grease a 20cm (8 in) cake tin.

Put the chocolate, broken into pieces, in a bowl, and place over a pan of simmering water. Leave until it has melted. Stir in the butter, 25g (1 oz) at a time, and combine well. Remove the bowl from the heat and stir in the sugar. Cool slightly, then beat in the egg yolks, flour, ground nuts, vanilla essence and orange rind.

Whisk the egg whites until soft peaks form and fold into the chocolate mixture. Spoon it into the cake tin and bake for 40 minutes. Leave to cool in the tin for 10 minutes before turning out on to a wire cooling rack.

When completely cold, cut the cake in half and sandwich together with raspberries and cream.

For extra chocolatiness, spread one half of the cake with melted white or plain chocolate in addition to the cream and raspberries.

Chocolate Crème Brûlée

These individual brûlées can be made two or three days in advance, but the sugar topping is best done only 2–3 hours before serving. Wonderful served on their own, but especially good if served with a bowl of strawberries, raspberries or cherries cooked in a little sugar syrup.

Serves 4-6

110G (4 OZ) PLAIN CHOCOLATE	4 EGG YOLKS
275ML (½ PINT) DOUBLE CREAM	1 TBSP SOFT BROWN SUGAR
150ML (¼ PINT) SINGLE CREAM	DEMERARA SUGAR, FOR TOPPING
½ TSP VANILLA ESSENCE	

Preheat the oven to 180°C/350°F/Gas 4.

Melt the chocolate, broken into pieces, in a small bowl over a pan of simmering water. Bring the creams and vanilla essence to boiling point, but don't allow it to boil. Stir in the melted chocolate.

Beat the egg yolks and soft brown sugar together. In a thin stream, stir in the chocolate cream mixture.

Pour the mixture into individual ramekins. Stand the ramekins in a baking tin and add enough boiling water to come half-way up the sides of the ramekins. Bake in the oven for 15–20 minutes. Remove the ramekins from the tin and allow to cool.

To serve, sprinkle demerara sugar in a thick layer over the chocolate brûlée and put under a preheated grill until the sugar caramelizes. Watch this procedure carefully as the sugar has a tendency to burn very quickly.

Chocolate and Raspberry Cake Mousse

A recipe that uses up leftover chocolate cake; plain sponge would work, too. The raspberries can be replaced with chopped cherries, peaches or strawberries.

Serves 6-8

50G (2 OZ) GOOD QUALITY CHOCOLATE	150ML (¼ PINT) DOUBLE CREAM
2 EGGS, SEPARATED	225G (8 OZ) RASPBERRIES
50G (2 OZ) CASTER SUGAR	EXTRA WHIPPED CREAM AND WHOLE RASPBERRIES
GRATED RIND OF 1 SMALL ORANGE	(OPTIONAL), TO DECORATE
2 TBSP FRESH ORANGE JUICE	
3 THICK SLICES CHOCOLATE CAKE, DICED	

Melt the chocolate, broken into pieces, in a bowl over a pan of simmering water. Beat the egg yolks and sugar together until they are pale and fluffy. Stir in the melted chocolate, then fold in the orange rind and juice and the diced cake.

In separate bowls, whisk the egg whites until they are stiff but not dry and beat the cream until it holds its shape. With a large metal spoon, carefully fold the cream and egg whites into the mousse mixture. Layer the mousse and raspberries in a serving bowl or individual glasses.

Decorate with extra whipped cream and whole raspberries, if liked.

Try using Cointreau or Grand Marnier instead of orange juice.

Chocolate and Almond Freezer Pudding

A good pudding to make if you want to get ahead with dinner party preparations. It is great served on its own with whipped cream, and extra special if you have a bowl of fresh strawberry or raspberry sauce to pass around separately.

Serves 6-8

75G (3 OZ) CASTER SUGAR	I SMALL EGG, BEATEN
75G (3 OZ) UNSALTED BUTTER, SOFTENED	75G (3 OZ) RATAFIA OR AMARETTI BISCUITS, ROUGHLY CRUMBLED
75G (3 OZ) DRINKING CHOCOLATE POWDER	WHIPPED CREAM AND GRATED CHOCOLATE OR TOASTED FLAKED ALMONDS, TO DECORATE
75G (3 OZ) GROUND ALMONDS	

Line a 450g (1 lb) loaf tin with clingfilm or lightly oil an 870ml (1½ pint) bowl.

In a pan, heat the sugar with 2 tablespoons of water until the sugar has dissolved. Allow to cool. Cream the butter and chocolate powder together, then stir in the ground almonds.

Gradually add the sugar syrup to the butter mixture, mixing well. Add the egg gradually, then beat again until light and creamy.

Add the crumbled biscuits to the mixture. Spoon into the prepared tin or bowl and press the mixture down well. Cover and freeze.

To serve, thaw at room temperature for 45 minutes, then turn out on to a serving plate and decorate with whipped cream and grated chocolate, or toasted flaked almonds.

Raspberry or Strawberry Sauce

Whizz together 225g (8 oz) of strawberries or raspberries with 25g (1 oz) of icing sugar and the juice of half an orange. Sieve the raspberry sauce if you prefer it seedless.

Chocolate Cheesecake

A moist coffee and chocolate cheesecake, which keeps well in the fridge for 3 or 4 days and can be frozen.

Serves 6-8

Base

75G (3 OZ) UNSALTED BUTTER	50G (2 OZ) CRUSHED HAZELNUTS,
175G (6 OZ) DIGESTIVES, CRUSHED	TOASTED

Filling

175G (6 OZ) COTTAGE CHEESE	110-175G (4-6 OZ) GOOD QUALITY
175G (6 OZ) CREAM CHEESE	PLAIN CHOCOLATE
150ML (¼ PINT) SOURED CREAM	1 TBSP CORNFLOUR, SIFTED
2 EGGS	2 TBSP STRONG COFFEE OR TIA
110G (4 OZ) SOFT BROWN SUGAR	MARIA

Preheat the oven to 170°C/325°F/Gas 3.

Melt the butter and stir in the crushed biscuits and nuts. Press into a 20cm (8 in) buttered spring-form or loose-bottomed cake tin. Chill for 30 minutes.

For the filling, sieve the cottage cheese into a large bowl, or whizz in a food processor until smooth. Beat in the cream cheese and soured cream. In a separate bowl, beat together the eggs and sugar until they are fluffy and light, then gradually stir into the cheese mixture.

Put the chocolate, broken up, into a bowl over a pan of simmering water, and leave until it has melted. Stir the chocolate into the cheese mixture, add the coffee or Tia Maria, add the sifted cornflour and stir well. Pour into the biscuit-lined tin and bake in the oven for 1¼ hours. Turn the oven off and leave the cheesecake in the oven overnight if possible or, alternatively, for 3-4 hours.

Remove the cheesecake from the tin and put on a serving dish. Chill for 2 hours. Serve with a bowl of crème fraîche.

Note

Soured cream can be made by adding 1 tablespoon of lemon juice to 150ml (¼ pint) of double cream.

Chocolate Pye

Pye is an old spelling of the more familiar word, which was in use when this dessert became popular. In it, a chocolate crust encases a rich creamy filling.

Serves 4-6

Base

110G (4 OZ) PLAIN FLOUR	110G (4 OZ) UNSALTED BUTTER,
25G (1 OZ) COCOA POWDER	DICED
½ TSP SALT	3 TBSP COLD WATER
75G (3 OZ) CASTER SUGAR	

Filling

275ML (½ PINT) SINGLE CREAM	1 TBSP BAILEYS, BRANDY OR RUM
225G (8 OZ) GOOD QUALITY	WHIPPED DOUBLE CREAM, TOASTED
CHOCOLATE	ALMONDS AND GRATED
275ML (½ PINT) DOUBLE CREAM	CHOCOLATE, TO DECORATE

Preheat the oven to 200°C/400°F/Gas 6.

To make the base, mix the flour, cocoa, salt and sugar, then rub in the butter until the mixture resembles fine breadcrumbs. Slowly add the water, until the mixture forms a ball. Allow to rest in the fridge for 30 minutes, wrapped in clingfilm. Bring the dough out to room temperature for 15-20 minutes, then roll it out between sheets of parchment paper and turn into a 20cm (8 in) flan tin. Prick all over with a fork. Put the flan tin on a preheated baking tray and bake in the oven for 15-20 minutes. Allow to cool on a wire cooling rack.

For the filling, heat the single cream and chocolate, broken

up, in a bowl over a pan of simmering water until the chocolate has melted. Remove from the heat and allow to cool for 15-20 minutes. Whisk the mixture vigorously until it is frothy. Place the chocolate crust on a serving dish and pour in the chocolate cream.

Refrigerate for 30-40 minutes. Decorate the pye with whipped cream, almonds and chocolate.

Chocolate and Apricot Cake

A very rich chocolate cake that is a wonderful dessert for chocolate-lovers.

Serves 6-8

Cake

50G (2 OZ) NO-SOAK APRICOTS, CHOPPED	150G (5 OZ) CASTER SUGAR
	200G (7 OZ) PLAIN CHOCOLATE
55ML (2 FL OZ) APRICOT BRANDY, BRANDY OR RUM	110G (4 OZ) UNSALTED BUTTER
	50G (2 OZ) PLAIN FLOUR
3 EGGS, SEPARATED	75G (3 OZ) GROUND ALMONDS

Icing

150ML (¼ PINT) DOUBLE CREAM	110G (4 OZ) WHITE CHOCOLATE
1 TBSP ICING SUGAR, SIFTED	1 TSP VANILLA ESSENCE

Preheat the oven to 180°C/350°F/Gas 4.

To make the cake, soak the apricots in the liqueur overnight.

Lightly oil and line a deep 20cm (8 in) cake tin with greaseproof or parchment paper.

Beat the egg yolks and sugar until they are pale and fluffy. Put the chocolate, broken up, and 2 tablespoons of water in a bowl over a pan of simmering water. When the chocolate has melted, stir in the butter, 25g (1 oz) at a time. Pour into the egg yolk mixture, stirring, then carefully fold in the flour, almonds and apricots.

Whisk the egg whites until they are stiff but not dry and fold them into the chocolate mixture. Pour into the prepared tin and bake in the oven for 30-40 minutes. Remove when the centre is still moist. Allow to cool in the tin, then remove to a serving plate.

Prepare the icing the day before you serve the cake.

In a pan, bring the cream and sugar to a simmer, then remove from the heat and stir in the white chocolate, broken into pieces. Stir until the chocolate has melted. Pour into a bowl, cover and refrigerate. Just before serving, stir the vanilla essence into the white chocolate.

Lime Pie
with Chocolate Icing

A variation of the American Key Lime Pie, which is so simple to make. You could substitute a biscuit base for the chocolate pastry.

Serves 4-6

Chocolate Pastry, see Chocolate Pye (page 123)

Filling

125ML (4 FL OZ) LIME JUICE	3 EGG YOLKS
1 X 400G (14 OZ) CAN CONDENSED MILK	

Icing

150G (5 OZ) PLAIN CHOCOLATE	150ML (¼ PINT) DOUBLE CREAM

Preheat the oven to 180°C/350°F/Gas 4.

Line a 20cm (8 in) pie tin with chocolate pastry and prebake (see Chocolate Pye, page 123).

Beat together the lime juice, condensed milk and egg yolks until smooth. Pour the batter into the pastry case and bake in the oven for 15 minutes. Allow to cool.

For the icing, heat the chocolate, broken up, and cream in a pan until the chocolate has melted and stir until the mixture is smooth. Allow to cool and thicken to a coating consistency. Pour over the pie and allow to harden for 2 hours.

Index